HOPE
for a
Woman's
Heart

Loura Nolt

ISBN: 978-1-63813-209-7

Cover and text layout design: Kristi Yoder

Printed in China

Published by:
TGS International
P.O. Box 355
Berlin, Ohio 44610 USA
Phone: 330.893.4828
Fax: 330-893-4893
www.tgsinternational.com

25 stories to inspire a closer walk with God

HOPE
for a
Woman's
Heart

Loura Nolt

Dedication

I'd like to dedicate this book to the many women who have touched my life in different ways—and to all women. Each of us leaves an impact; may your impact be one of blessing and hope!

Table of Contents

Acknowledgments

*M*y deepest thanks belongs to my heavenly Father for His goodness to me—for His love, His forgiveness, His mercy, and His grace. As I reflect on all that He is to me, Psalm 28:7 comes to mind: "The LORD is my strength and my shield; my heart trusted in him, and I am helped: therefore my heart greatly rejoiceth; and with my song will I praise him."

To each of the following, I would also like to say a heartfelt "Thank you!"

- First of all, to my dear husband Carl for your love and patience as I write and process life through my fingers on my keyboard. You are so good for me. Your love and steady support mean so much. Your ability to know what to say, and when, is incredible when I consider how my brain can jump from one thing to the next too quickly. May God bless you in your dedication to being a godly father and husband. And may our years together continue to be beautiful as we walk through them one day at a time.

- To my six lovely children: Seth, Leah, Grace, Adam, Anne, and Emma. Each one of you is the light of my life. I love you all the "best," and my prayer is that of 3 John 1:4: "I have no greater joy than to hear that my children walk in truth." Thank you for being my sweetest collection of "fans" and allowing me to share my heart through my writing. May God be your closest Friend as you walk through whatever lies ahead for you. And always remember—your mother loves you so much.

- To both of my mothers—Elizabeth and Anna—my mom and my husband's mom. Your example and love in raising your children has inspired me in many ways as I strive to mimic the good you have done. You are so good to me and so wonderful to my children. God bless you and may you continue to be faithful to stand for the truth.

- To my sisters and friends—those women to whom I owe so much. You are such a blessing to me! Thank you for your support and for helping me with ideas and suggestions when I needed them.

- To the editing and publishing team at TGS—you were amazing to work with and so personable. From discussions of birds to Pennsylvania Dutch, it has all been such a positive experience for me! May God bless your work as you strive to publish hope and truth for God.

- To my friend and fellow writer, Donna, for all your time spent proofreading, critiquing, and encouraging me to keep on writing. God bless you.

Introduction

"*Hope is being able to see that there is light beyond the darkness, and hills beyond the valleys.*" —Author unknown

I read this quote and immediately my mind went to a favorite verse in Habakkuk: "Although the fig tree shall not blossom, neither shall fruit be in the vines; the labour of the olive shall fail, and the fields shall yield no meat; the flock shall be cut off from the fold, and there shall be no herd in the stalls: Yet I will rejoice in the LORD, I will joy in the God of my salvation. The LORD God is my strength, and he will make my feet like hinds' feet, and he will make me to walk upon mine high places" (Habakkuk 3:17–19).

Every time I read this verse, I think of "high places" and how I long for them.

This past summer I experienced lots of high places. We took a once-in-a-lifetime family trip to see the West. The mountains are so beautiful—and incredibly high.

I couldn't get done exclaiming over them—or telling my husband to "stay over" as we drove the winding switchbacks with no guardrails. When I was done hyperventilating, I really did enjoy it. I only hoped we would get to the top alive.

I grew up in the mountains of Pennsylvania, but those mountains are mere hills compared to the Colorado Rockies. The feeling of standing on those high places, looking far out over the valleys below, was like none I had ever before experienced. After I rallied myself and caught my breath from the drive up, I felt the tears sting my eyes as I took in the beauty of what lay in front of us.

It was more than I had hoped for! God surely has created some awesome high places.

Sometimes life as a woman in today's complicated world is like an unplanned trip. We need to hang on to faith and hope through the entire trip. And since we get only one lifetime, it's a once-in-a-lifetime trip.

We can go from the heights of emotional mountains to the depths of dark valleys of discouragement in a short span of time (sometimes minutes, if you are anything like me), depending on what situations we are facing. Life's pathway from valley to mountain can be just as difficult as the one our family took on those winding, unguarded roads. If I lose hope in the valleys, I can become lost and discouraged.

As women, we can get caught up in a valley of worry for the future, as well as an overwhelming sense of never being quite enough—not enough for all the work we need to do, not enough for our children, not enough for our husbands . . . our friends . . . The list goes on. As we give in to surrounding pressures, our hope tends to slip away. We seem to be in a valley with no mountaintop in sight.

My friend, don't ever lose HOPE. Remember, God wants to walk with us through the valleys. For every valley He takes us through, He has a future mountaintop to show us. He has given us so much hope. With Him, I can walk safely through the valleys and on to the high places.

No matter the difficulties you are up against—and I know, sometimes life gets really hard—the secret to finding those high places is to hold on to HOPE in Christ. Then, with hope, we look for joy in the journey and cling to the God of our salvation.

My prayer is that when you take this book in hand, no matter what you are facing, you will find hope to look onward to the high places God has for you.

Search for Him. Cling to Him in the valleys. And when you get to the high places, throw up your hands in adoration and let the tears of thankfulness flow. It will be more than you ever hoped for! You are a beautiful creation, made for His glory, and He has a plan for every valley and every mountaintop you encounter in your life. You can live with hope unmeasured!

Walk with me, my friend, and as you read each story may you be inspired to hold on to hope—to be able to praise God in the valleys as well as the high places. Though I have much more to learn, God is teaching me so much. And it is with hope that I set my face forward.

His promises for us are sure and steadfast. Hope in Him!

CHAPTER ONE

Hope—At Just the Right Time

Now the God of hope fill you with all joy and peace in believing, that ye may abound in hope, through the power of the Holy Ghost. Romans 15:13

*E*ven if I hadn't seen the unique cap on her head, the dark circles under her eyes told the story.

Pain.

The lack of hair, the pale skin, it all spoke of a woman facing an intense battle.

Cancer. Chemotherapy.

I was at a pottery shop where you can buy unpainted pottery and then use their supplies to paint something on it. The lady pulled out a piece of pottery I had painted and commented, "It seems like I keep seeing sayings just when I need them most." Her gaze was fixed on a plate I had painted with the words, "It will not always be the way it is now."

Her stance and body, though obviously battling for health, gave off vibes of courageous positivity. "That is a good thing to remember," she said. "I need to keep praying." She held the platter as if it were a vessel offering hope.

Later, as I stood along the wall trying to figure out which colors to choose for the project I was working on, I heard her singing. Words of praise floated from her lips, and out of the corner of my eye I saw her face.

It stirred my heart.

In her pain, her battle for life, she was making a deliberate choice. Her attitude inspired me. Beneath the smile and the words she was singing, I could see deep pain in her heart. Yet she was being so brave.

But it was her eyes that really touched me.

Then I wondered—would I have noticed them if it hadn't been for her lack of hair and pale skin? Would I have seen the pain?

I know I have missed many opportunities over the years to bring hope to a hurting heart because I was too self-focused to see the pain.

As a mother, I have at times misinterpreted eyes of sadness as a lack of motivation. By doing so, I have callously ignored a hurting heart. Maybe my insensitivity has even caused the hurt I sometimes see in the eyes of my children.

I should know better.

I have a sensitive heart myself and have often tried to mask pain underneath laughter and an outgoing personality. What a blessing to have those close to me see through the facade. These sweet friends gently point out the pain and encourage me to face it. They are blessed vessels of hope to me.

"What is your name?" I hesitantly asked the lady after I paid my bill. I was afraid she would think me too forward, but I wanted to know so I could personally pray for her.

There are so many opportunities to love and care for hearts. So many chances to spread hope.

"I'm Robin," she smiled.

"I'll pray for you, Robin," I said, swallowing the emotion in my throat.

"Thank you," she replied. "We can never have too much prayer." Her voice had a firmness that showed she really believed it. I left the shop with the look in her eyes still piercing my heart.

I may never see Robin again. I may never know the outcome of her cancer battle on this side of heaven. But I can pray for her. And I know God can do more for her than I or any doctor or medication can do. He can offer hope. The hope that really matters.

There are folks I *will* see though. My husband. My children. My friends. There are so many opportunities to love and care for hearts. So many chances to spread hope.

As I get older, I pray for discernment to see past the masks people wear to cover their hearts. I also pray for willingness to be brave and face my own pain—no matter how difficult—and to hold on to the hand of God, believing He is in total control.

To the hurting around me, I want to offer the message of hope painted on the plate: "It will not always be the way it is now." That quote is so full of meaning—in more ways than one.

If we are in deep pain, facing loss, illness, or heartache, it offers hope that things will get better. If we are experiencing joy and sweet blessings, it reminds us to treasure each moment because life is short. If we are in the prime of life, it is a reminder that all too soon we will be among the old.

Times change. My children will grow up, and I will no longer rock my babies in my good old rocking chair. My husband and I will change from young to old and be surprised at the rapid pace of the passing years.

I want the ability to see deeper than the surface in those I love. To do that, I must understand my own feelings and emotions. And most of all, I must have discernment to recognize when God is nudging me to offer His hope to others.

I can never do it on my own. But with His help, I can be a vessel of hope.

At just the right time.

CHAPTER TWO

Tangled in Briars

Jesus saith unto him, I am the way, the truth, and the life: no man cometh unto the Father, but by me. John 14:6

It was getting cold.

After being in the tree stand for several hours, I decided it was time to head back to the house for a break.

For me, hunting is primarily something I do for my family—though it's not that I dislike it. As our children have grown older, both the boys and the girls have shown an interest in hunting. We soon realized my husband couldn't help everyone, so I took my hunter safety course and joined the ranks of the orange clad when hunting season rolled around each year.

My son was in a tree stand nearby, so I thought I'd take a round-about path to the house in hopes of scaring up some deer for him. It seemed like a great idea.

I started down what looked like an unobstructed path heading in the direction I wanted to go. Through the trees, I could easily see our house and shop.

I wasn't walking long until I came to a brushy area. Looking around, I found a place I could get through, but the briars were nasty and getting worse. Thankful to be properly clothed with my husband's heavy hunting clothing, I pushed through as the briars grabbed at my clothing. I worked hard to keep them out of my face, the only uncovered spot. Soon, however, I came to a thicket of briars and small trees so dense there was absolutely no way for me to pass through.

I stopped and stared into the brush. *Come on,* I thought. *The house is right over there. Surely I can find a way through.*

But no, there was simply no opening big enough to squeeze through, though I checked everywhere.

There was nothing to do but go back. Climbing back up the hill was harder than coming down. I couldn't even see the places where I had pushed through the briars minutes before. This time they yanked off my hood, grabbed me tighter, and seemed reluctant to let go.

What was I thinking? I wondered as I pushed on. *This was not a good idea. If there are any deer here, they can just stay!*

Partway back to where I had started, I glanced to my left and saw the trail I should have taken. *Maybe I could cut across through the brush to the trail,* I thought. *Then I won't have to go all the way back to the tree stand.*

I started through the brush toward the trail. It was hard going, and I soon had to get down on my hands and knees to crawl under some branches. I lost my orange hat and felt my skirt tear.

Back on my feet, I glanced ahead. Between me and the trail

was a huge fallen tree, surrounded by briars so thick I saw no way through. Desperately I glanced behind me where I had already pushed through—and that now looked impassable as well.

There was nowhere to go but over the fallen tree. Holding my gun above my head, I stumbled and tripped and climbed my way over the tree, wondering if anyone would ever find me if I got hung up and couldn't move. I knew I was within shouting distance of the house if I got stuck, but envisioning the expression of disbelief and humor on my husband's face kept me struggling to fight my way through.

I won't let anyone find me here, I thought, fighting down a feeling of panic.

That's when it started to rain.

Perfect, I thought sarcastically. Now I was not only cold, miserable, and nearly stuck, but I was getting wet.

Muttering to myself, I struggled on. Finally I broke through the last branch and found myself on the open trail.

I looked back to see where I had come through and had to laugh aloud. *Wow*, I thought, *am I ever glad no one was around to watch me flounder through that mess!* Especially when just a few yards away lay a nice open trail with no briars.

After adjusting my clothes and checking for damage, I was soon on my way to the house, walking freely with nothing but mud to slow me down.

I shook my head. *Okay, Loura, that wasn't the brightest thing you have ever done.*

I could have saved myself a lot of aggravation by simply following the clearly marked trail. Yes, I had something good in mind—chasing a deer to my son—but after a while that goal had faded as

I floundered around.

Life is all about choices. Some we make carelessly or with little thought; others we struggle and pray through. But each decision leads us in one direction or another. Some may be drastic turns on the trail of life, while others are simply a gradual shift in direction. But even these gradual shifts can throw our long-term goal off course and totally change the outcome.

Sometimes they lead us to a wall of briars. *How did I get here?* we wonder. *Why did I ever allow myself to go this direction in the first place?*

Maybe it's a bad habit or an unhealthy lifestyle choice. Or maybe it's the gradual callousing of our mother-heart, and we say things that should never be said by a Christian mom. We resort to scolding and shaming instead of patience and a bridled tongue.

Or we gradually allow ourselves to become more and more domineering with our husband, pushing against him when we should be honoring his leadership. One day we realize we have become entangled in a nasty briar patch of being a rebellious wife. Something we said we'd never be.

That's just where Satan wants us. Maybe he can't snare us in the big things, but little by little he dulls our awareness of our actions and where they might lead. Unhealthy thought patterns, unkind words, gossip, discontentment, selfish choices—they entangle us and try to pull us further in.

> The choice is mine. I must recognize where I am, examine my life, and take the necessary steps to get back on the right path—with God's help.

Then, when we realize where we are and how far off the God-path we've gone, Satan hits us with a shower of hopelessness and despair. "You can't do it. You always mess up. Look at you, all caught up in this sin. If people would know! There's no way out. You're a failure." I think of 1 Peter 5:8, which shows the true colors of Satan: "Be sober, be vigilant; because your adversary the devil, as a roaring lion, walketh about, seeking whom he may devour."

Satan has no limits to his blows, except when we call upon Jesus, and then he has no strength at all. The choice is mine. I must recognize where I am, examine my life, and take the necessary steps to get back on the right path—with God's help.

When I was floundering through the briars, I kept looking through the trees to keep my sights on the house, not wanting to get too far off course. And that's how it must be in my life. I must keep my eyes on Jesus. If I keep Him in my sights, I will be okay. If I lose sight of my Lord, I will only see the briars around me and become discouraged.

This story could be symbolic of salvation as well. There is only one way to heaven—through Jesus. All other ways will lead to tangled vines and deceptive pathways. These may look easy and right at first, but they end up entangling us so tightly we cannot find a way out.

In John 14:6, Jesus said, "I am the way, the truth, and the life: no man cometh unto the Father, but by me."

Jesus' way is the only way. Let Him pull you from the briars and set you back on the pathway that leads HOME.

I didn't get a deer or even see one that day, but I learned a valuable lesson about walking with the Lord. Stay on the right path and keep focused on the goal. Beware of deceptive pathways. And be willing to backtrack and start over when necessary.

It will make all the difference in the world.

CHAPTER THREE

Sweeter Than Cake

Therefore all things whatsoever ye would that men should do to you, do ye even so to them: for this is the law and the prophets. Matthew 7:12

We have been selling puppies for a few years now, and most of the time I thoroughly enjoy it. It is a good family project, for we all love puppies. The advertising, emailing, and phone calls take time, but when a happy puppy customer leaves our home with a new pet and a smile, it makes it all worthwhile.

One day a new customer came to our home to see a litter of puppies. They knew the puppies were not ready to go yet but wanted to pick out one. The correspondence had been by email, so we didn't know much about the people. The lady did write that this was their first pet, that they did not have a family, and that her husband worked for the state.

When they pulled in that evening, I was a little surprised by their appearance. I think they were not sure about me either. In very broken English, she introduced herself and her husband. They appeared to be of Indian descent.

As we brought them into the house and showed them our five pug puppies, they chattered to each other in their own language. I felt a little disconcerted, not sure if I should stay there or step back and give them time with the puppies. Sometimes the lady would switch to English and ask a question or two. I struggled to understand and wasn't always sure she understood me.

Puppy customers often comment on or interact with our children, who are always right there, but this couple barely noticed them. I can typically read people, but with these folks I had no idea how they were feeling. I couldn't even tell if they liked our puppies! They finally asked about a deposit, and with many hand gestures and repeated questions we got things figured out. They picked out a puppy, wrote a check, and left with a promise to return in two weeks to pick it up.

I was skeptical. I wasn't sure if I trusted the check or if they would return. I even wondered if they might come back some dark night and rob us!

The check cleared, however, and the lady contacted me with a few questions over the next two weeks. Everything seemed okay, but I was still uncertain. I didn't think I was the type of person to judge others by their descent or skin color, but now I questioned myself, *Loura, what is your problem?*

On the day they planned to arrive, we bathed their puppy and got it ready. As they came up the walk, the lady's face broke into a big smile—the first real smile I had seen on her. "So excited!" she said as she made clapping motions.

They gave me the rest of the money in cash, and we signed the papers. All the while they chattered to each other in their own language, and I felt like an unlearned toddler.

I noticed her motioning to our children while saying something to her husband. He nodded and said to me, "Be back—have gift."

As he raced out the door to their vehicle, she smiled at me. While huggIng her puppy, she said, "So excited for puppy, we forget gift!" and shook her head. I was confused. *Gift?*

In a few minutes her husband was back, carrying a cake. He handed it to me and said, "For kids. They like? They eat?" He looked so hopeful and nervous, glancing from me to the cake to the children.

Astounded at their sweetness, I hardly knew what to say. "For us?" I exclaimed. "Oh, thank you. Yes! They will eat it. They love cake!"

Again the woman clapped her hands, her face alight in a beautiful smile. In her broken English, she told me how they had stopped at two stores on their way looking for something for our children but were nervous about what we would like. "We think, 'Kids like cake.' So we get cake."

I was so blessed! Thanking them again, I gave her a hug. Before I knew it, they were gone, and there on my table sat a lovely chocolate cake with fudge icing. My children wanted to enjoy it immediately, so I got plates. They ran excitedly for Daddy, and we had a little cake party right then and there.

These people were the last ones I would have dreamed would bring a cake for us when they showed up for their puppy. What a blessing they had been!

It was a good lesson for me. We should never assume something about people before we give them a chance to show who they truly are. I will certainly try to be more open-minded in the future!

As God's people, we should be more accepting than those who don't know Him. No matter who the person is, every human being is created and loved by God. And He wants me to love and accept anyone He brings across my path.

As I pondered that concept, my mind turned to our relationships within the body of Christ. How quickly we misunderstand each other! We may see or hear something about someone and quickly form an opinion—passing judgment before we hear both sides of the story. This is devastating to relationships! I think of James 3:10: "Out of the same mouth proceedeth blessing and cursing. My brethren, these things ought not so to be."

I think that cake was the sweetest cake I have ever eaten. And it wasn't the sugar. It was the lesson and the blessing that went with it.

CHAPTER FOUR

A Belch of Steam

Be sober, be vigilant; because your adversary the devil, as a roaring lion, walketh about, seeking whom he may devour. 1 Peter 5:8

My face was likely glowing as brightly as the taillights. The "Behemoth" had become a fire-breathing dragon—and I was behind the wheel!

The old school van is truly a Perry County redneck type of vehicle. One by one this fell off, that stopped working, and something else dragged. But it still ran, and if we took it to the right place it even passed inspection! But I didn't mind its rattles and idiosyncrasies.

Until today.

It was my week to drive the children to school. I knew there were some slight problems with this beast of a van the scholars had named the "Behemoth." Recently every time it came to a stop, it let out a puff of steam that rolled up from the hood and over the windshield.

It also emitted an unpleasant odor. But it had been doing that for a few years now . . .

My husband checked it over and didn't seem too concerned. "Someone must have filled the radiator too full and water is sloshing out, causing that cloud of steam," he said. "It should be fine. Just don't take it too far." There did seem to be a small leak in a hose somewhere, but hey, as long as it fired up and moved when I put it into gear, it was good enough for me.

I pulled into the drive-through at the bank after dropping off the scholars and was embarrassed by the clouds of steam the teller commented on. There was a problem with my deposits, so I told her I would come back later in the day. "If this thing still moves, that is," I joked.

> If I hear that "still small voice" nudging me, am I willing to stop and check what is wrong, or do I ignore it and barrel on until the steam is rolling and I have created a real problem?

When I pulled into the drive-through again that afternoon, I saw the same teller at the window. "Hey, it's still running!" I grinned. But the longer I sat there, the more I began to doubt if it really was okay.

As I continued toward school to pick up the children, the steam suddenly got a LOT worse. Soon the inside of the van was steamed up, and I was afraid the whole thing was going to blow up or burst into flames!

And I was right in the center of our nosy little town.

Seeing an alley to my right, I pulled off the road and shut down the engine. I bailed out of the van, tears streaming from my eyes because of the thick steam coming through the vents. If I thought it had been steaming before, the Behemoth was really angry now. The steam rolling from under the hood was so thick I couldn't see the front of the van.

Now what?

Looking left and right, I longed to find a rock big enough to crawl under. I considered (briefly) standing on the sidewalk and pretending to be a tongue-clicking observer. *I wonder who would drive such a wreck. Don't they know that thing should be run off a cliff somewhere?*

Suddenly I recognized a truck pulling into the alley. *Ahh . . . help!* In the form of a grandpa from our church. He soon had the hood open and was checking out things. I called for backup to collect our scholars at school, ducking my head as I watched a few school vans zip by—vans that ran nicely and didn't give out bursts of embarrassing steam.

Grandpa's head soon emerged from the steam with a diagnosis: the radiator was dry.

So that was the problem! My husband had filled it the night before and thought it would be fine. "Didn't the gauge show that the engine was hot?" my rescuing angel asked.

"Well, no," I said sheepishly. "The gauges don't work."

With a radiator full of fresh water and the help of my kind rescuer, I was able to start the van and drive home. As humiliating as it was, I had a grin on my face.

You see, I kind of like this old van.

After years of being a faithful school van, it has become a real conversation piece. I mean, no one else drives such a beauty—no tint, paint chipping, and with a unique rumble and smell. The van is actually older than one of the mothers on our school route!

I started imagining what it would be like if we got a new vehicle to drive the schoolchildren. Would I even know how to read the gauges? Would I trust them to tell me what's going on under the hood? Or would I ignore them because I had learned that I cannot count on gauges?

What about my own "gauges"?

As a child of God, I have been given specific gauges to keep myself on the pathway my Father has in mind for me. One of these gauges is my conscience. If I hear that "still small voice" nudging me, am I willing to stop and check what is wrong, or do I ignore it and barrel on until the steam is rolling and I have created a real problem?

Maybe I have become lax with my children or allowed anger and impatience to creep into my voice. Maybe I've become a bit lazy with my housework or allowed myself to become unmotivated or careless with my health. Consequently, I feel lethargic and overweight, suffering from health-related frustrations. Or maybe I have gotten off track reading things that aren't helpful in Christian living or become distracted with technology and am ignoring my family.

Does my world need to steam dramatically to get my attention? Or am I in tune enough with God to see the red light on the gauge and then stop to take a good look at where I am going before it is too late?

Do I listen to my husband (he is a God-given gauge in my life) when he sees an area that needs work? Am I open to the advice of others who care about me?

As Christian women, we have a high calling in a distracting world. If we are busy, preoccupied, and not in touch with our spiritual gauges, we suffer and lose our way in finding the heart of God. It brings tears to my eyes when I think of how Satan wants to ruin our gauges and bring suffering to those close to us.

My heart trembles as I come before my Father with an ache inside: *Lord, please fine-tune my sensitivity to the gauges you have given me. Help me hear your voice and stay close to you. Please help me see myself for who I really am.*

I may be a bit worn for the wear. Like the Behemoth, I may even be a conversation piece, someone others may not really understand. I may not be the most popular, and I may even be rejected or disrespected at times.

But if I am in the center of God's will for me, I am of much more value than any old Behemoth school van.

CHAPTER FIVE

The Tugboat Tongue

Even so the tongue is a little member, and boasteth great things. Behold, how great a matter a little fire kindleth! James 3:5

We watched in fascination as the huge barge in front of us was slowly being lowered.

We had stopped beside the muddy Mississippi River, almost a thousand miles from home, to stretch our legs and hopefully release some bound-up energy. We were delighted to find a barge within the lock and in the process of being lowered when we arrived. The timing couldn't have been better.

As we stood alongside the chain-link fence under the highway bridge, my husband explained to the children what was taking place. We marveled at this amazing man-made structure that could raise and lower boats from one section of the river to the next. The wind whipped past us and tousled our hair, already messy from the long all-night drive. The morning sun was warm and the day beautiful.

Finally the barge was level with the lower part of the river. Slowly the gates opened and the long, loaded barge eased out toward the current, right in front of us.

"What makes it move?" one of the children wondered.

"Just wait and see," my husband answered.

We soon saw how the barge was moving. A tugboat, with its motor revved up, was right behind it, pushing it along. It was incredible. The size of the tugboat compared to the barge was almost like an ant and an elephant, and yet the little boat was doing an amazing job. It wasn't long until the barge was out in the current and moving downstream away from us.

"That little boat must be very strong!" someone exclaimed.

And it was. If the barge drifted one way, the tugboat gunned its engine to get it back on course. With a little effort, it changed the direction of the whole barge.

It reminded me of James 3:5: "Even so the tongue is a little member, and boasteth great things. Behold, how great a matter a little fire kindleth!"

Our tongues may be a small and hidden part of us, but oh, the things they can accomplish! The tongue is an indicator of the status of our hearts, whether good or evil.

With the tongue, we communicate among ourselves. We spread love and encouragement. Or we tear down and discourage. One little slip of the tongue in a negative or hurtful way can cause harm that may take a long time to heal.

Just like a tugboat, the tongue is a rudder, changing with the condition of our heart. Some days I find it easy to speak words of blessing and spread God's love in gentle and kind tones. But other days, when my patience is tested, I find myself responding with words that cut and destroy. As James 3:8 says, "But the tongue can no man tame; it is an unruly evil, full of deadly poison."

If anyone has ever spoken to you with sharp words, you can relate to the feeling of the tongue being evil. And if you have ever given in and lashed out at others with words that cut like a knife, you know how quickly this can happen and how badly you feel afterwards.

I have always admired people who take time to think before they speak. I am often the opposite—too quick to voice a thought, and then later regretting my choice of words. Too often I need to return with an apology. We are all human, but when we recognize a weakness in ourselves, we need to acknowledge it and allow God to shape us to become more like Him.

> The words we speak can make an incredible difference— for good or for evil.

Think of a little tugboat—how it can move a huge barge with ease. Have you ever been in a tense situation, and someone spoke words of wisdom at just the right time? The words we speak can make an incredible difference—for good or for evil.

We can use our tongue to twist words and create problems, or we can use it to pass on peace and kindness. The tongue is a little thing, but if we speak in godly ways it can bring joy in ways we can't imagine.

Recently I read an article on the power of suggestion. We might not necessarily speak an untruth but merely suggest something negative. This can create much confusion and hurt. It is one of Satan's ways to stir up dissension between friends or fellow believers. May we be careful not to get caught in this trap of using our tongue to stir up strife.

As the barge and the tugboat faded from sight, we turned and prepared to get back into the van for the remainder of our ride to Missouri. God uses many things to get our attention, and this time He used the tugboat to speak to me. I was convicted to guard my tongue—to be careful that the words and meditations of my heart are acceptable in His sight and will bring glory to Him.

God must be the Captain of my tugboat tongue!

CHAPTER SIX

From Rags to Rugs

And I will restore to you the years that the locust hath eaten. Joel 2:25

It's a real mess.

Glancing about my kitchen, I sigh emphatically as I roll up my sleeves and get busy. I tend to be a messy cook. I often give myself a sermon as I begin my work in the kitchen, but it seems inevitable. I just make a mess. By the time I finish baking or whipping up supper, I am bound to have flour splotched on my dress, some splatters here and there, and one or two utensils clattering to the floor.

I may be able to place my nouns and verbs in the proper order and write a grammatically correct article, but I am certainly not gifted in neat "cookmanship." I applaud any woman who cooks, bakes, or mixes things and does not spill, drip, or splash all around her. I keep thinking maybe someday I'll do better, but that day hasn't arrived yet.

As I kneel to clean up the cake batter that dripped on the floor, my eyes go to the rugs in my kitchen. Immediately my heart lightens. These rugs are so special! With their shades of blue, they match my kitchen with its blue tile countertop.

But it's not the color of the rugs that warms my heart. It's what they represent. It's because of the hands that handed them to me.

The rugs were a gift from dear friends in Virginia. Now they are a beautiful reminder of our friendship.

I like how rugs are made from rags. Old dresses, worn-out clothes, even jeans, turn from something useless into something very useful.

What looks to us like a stinking pile of rags can be the very thing God uses to bring more souls to freedom.

I'm not sure how it's done, but with some twisting and craftsmanship, something worn out is made into a thing of beauty to grace my kitchen floor.

Looking at the way the colors blend together speaks to me of careful consideration on the part of my friends. They took time to coordinate their rags into matching colors so the rugs would be beautiful, not just random colors.

I think of how God does the same for us. My righteousness is as filthy rags. Without His redemption, I have nothing to offer my Father but old rags.

One of my favorite verses is Isaiah 61:3: "To appoint unto them that mourn in Zion, to give unto them beauty for ashes, the oil of joy for mourning, the garment of praise for the spirit of heaviness; that they might be called trees of righteousness, the planting of the

LORD, that he might be glorified."

Only God can redeem my rags and turn them into beauty. I am eternally grateful for a Father who takes me as I am and then turns me into someone who can bring glory to Him.

What others may see as useless, God can turn into something useful. What looks to us like a stinking pile of rags can be the very thing God uses to bring more souls to freedom.

As I continue to clean up my messy kitchen, I think of another verse that has blessed me—Joel 2:25: "And I will restore to you the years that the locust hath eaten . . ."

I'm so thankful my Father is willing and able to take the rags of my life and use them to His honor and glory. All I need to do is recognize them as the rags they are and in humility bring them to the cross.

Now I take a step back; my kitchen is looking pretty good! It went from a mess . . . to order. God isn't the only one in the business of restoration. I just restored order to my kitchen as I pondered some deep truths. And it will stay that way—until I prepare the next meal!

Isn't this also how our Christian life works? It takes continual main-tenance to keep our hearts and minds free and ready for His service. I must stay immersed in His Word and abide in His presence.

So the next time I shake these rugs to remove the dust and dirt they have collected, I will remember that my "rags" can be made into beautiful "rugs" in the hands of my Father.

The words of a song float from my lips: "He's still working on me . . . to make me what I ought to be . . ."

CHAPTER SEVEN

Isaiah 53:5

But he was wounded for our transgressions, he was bruised for our iniquities: the chastisement of our peace was upon him; and with his stripes we are healed. Isaiah 53:5

"*B*ut he was wounded for our transgressions."

Wounded? That's an easy word to understand physically. Webster defines it as *an injury to living tissue caused by a cut, blow, or other impact; typically one in which the skin is cut or broken.*

We've all had wounds. As children, we no doubt experienced cuts, scrapes, and other bruises. Maybe we even had a traumatic wound that needed stitching or surgery.

And we all learned that wounds bring pain.

There is another definition for wound—a verb: *to inflict an injury on someone.* Yes, sometimes people do the wounding. Hopefully any physical injury we inflict on someone else is unintentional.

But I'm thinking of a deeper wounding. What about wounds of the heart? Those deep hidden wounds that fester, bleed, heal slowly, and cause so much emotional pain.

. . . .

The little girl knew Daddy was angry at her. She could tell by the crease in his brow, the scowl on his face. His strong arms moved roughly and quickly. What had she done? Somehow she must have made him angry. Cowering behind the door, she tried to vanish out of sight, hoping against hope he would soon walk away. She was afraid of his strength and his anger. She had felt it many times in her short life.

How was she to know he wasn't angry at HER? That his day had gone wrong, and he was just frustrated. But in that moment, she is wounded. Her little heart hurts as she carries a burden not her own.

> Physical bruises are visible and ugly. But heart bruises are nearly impossible to detect.

Only God can see the depths of such wounding. Tears fill His eyes as He weeps with a heart of compassion for the innocent children who suffer when self-absorbed adults don't care for their little hearts.

And He cares for the father as well. Within the father's heart are wounds no one may ever know.

But Jesus understands! He was beaten, and His skin was torn as the nails went through His hands and feet, and the spear entered His side. His heart was also wounded as He was despised, rejected, and mocked. He did it for me.

"He was bruised for our iniquities."

Bruises hurt. Ask anyone who's been kicked by a cow, fallen from a horse, been in a car accident, or even stubbed a toe. The black and blue marks are proof that damage has taken place. Physical bruises are visible and ugly. But heart bruises are nearly impossible to detect. Consider the following:

"So you had another miscarriage?"

The question pulled Miriam from her reverie with a jolt. Outside after church, she had been standing off to the side in silent pain.

"Yes . . ." she said hesitantly, reluctant to talk.

"At least you have three children," the older woman chirped. "Some people don't have any."

As the woman walked away, Miriam bit her lip and fought back the tears. The words had left a bruise on her heart. Oh, she knew they were true. She *was* blessed with three healthy children and was so very grateful. But she also had three babies in heaven, and her heart felt like it was bleeding.

What she needed were words of compassion and understanding. A gentle touch. Not a pat answer! No one knew the tears she cried as she tried in vain to be brave.

Or maybe the bruising comes another way:

"We heard some things about you and are very disappointed." In bewilderment, Jane tried to wrap her mind around the accusation. She knew where it had come from. No words could describe the pain of her struggling heart.

It wasn't true—those things they were saying—yet she could not defend herself every time the rumor mill spun. Her accusers seemed intent on believing the worst and making it sound so bad. The lies spun in her mind with such intensity that she declared within herself, *I'll never trust anyone again!*

The One who sees the wounds in the hearts of men and women sees Miriam and Jane's bruises as well. He knows Miriam's friend meant well and was only trying to ease the pain in the best way she knew. He knows Jane's accusers believe they are right, and that they have no idea of the devastation they have caused to her heart. But Jesus sees the whole picture!

Our bruises are His bruises. He understands. He was bruised for all the wrongs in the world. With His blood, He paid for every iniquity, every wrong.

And He was completely innocent. He was bruised for *our* iniquities.

. . . .

"The chastisement of our peace was upon him."

The absence of peace is turmoil. It is confusion, chaos—a disturbance of situations, circumstances, and individuals.

Shaking with cold, a young girl sits on the doctor's table. She is only a shell of what she was created to be. Because of her pain and her inability to release control of her life, she has been labeled anorexic. She is fully in bondage to it. She is so blinded she can't see her true situation.

For her there is no peace. Satan's lies about who she is and what she needs to do have confused her. The dark voices are in control, even as they lie to her.

But there is hope! Jesus gave His life so she could live in peace, free from Satan and his snares. Beautiful peace! There is no reason for her to punish herself.

If she could only see the Father's eyes of love for her, and see that He has paved the way for her to have peace. He can do this if she surrenders to His love.

So it is with all our sins. The only way to peace is by turning to Jesus—and away from ourselves and our own ways of pacifying the pain in our hearts. All our addictions—whether food, gossip, trying to manage everything, people pleasing, despondency, and more—can be overcome by the blood of the Lamb. Jesus is the Lamb of God who takes away the sin of the world. He has already accepted our punishment so we can have peace with God.

. . . .

"And with his stripes we are healed."

Healing is a miracle! The body mends itself and we take it for granted—until someone becomes terminally ill. Only then do we realize what a miracle physical healing is!

Physical healing is beautiful. But even more amazing is spiritual healing—the healing of deep wounds and ugly bruises. Jesus' blood heals them all.

Feeling the trembling in her heart, a young woman faces her offender, the one who caused such deep pain and years of guilt and shame. No, she doesn't feel completely at peace, but she has made a choice. She will forgive.

With conviction she says words she never thought she could: "I forgive you."

That is healing. No one can describe it until it is experienced. Satan tries to convince us that to forgive is to let the perpetrator off the hook. That it is saying what happened doesn't really matter.

Wrong.

Forgiveness is simply saying, "I will give you what God gave me. I didn't deserve His sacrifice, and neither do you deserve my forgiveness. But I will forgive because of Jesus." It is through this act of surrendering control that the chains are broken and our soul is set free.

God can only heal a soul that is willing to go all the way with Him. The stripes on His back make it possible for us to come to Him and experience healing for any emotional wounds in this sinful world.

By *His* stripes we are healed.

CHAPTER EIGHT

The Gift of a Sister

For ye have not received the spirit of bondage again to fear;
but ye have received the Spirit of adoption, whereby
we cry, Abba, Father. Romans 8:15

She came to us as a tiny, premature seven-week-old baby. Although she had no hair and eyes too big for her little face, she stole our hearts immediately. I will never forget the crying, crying, crying she did in her first weeks with us. She was a colicky baby, uprooted and in need of so much love.

I was a teenager at the time. Mom and Dad had been foster parents for a few years, and I wasn't very fond of the experience. It was hard to take care of these children and allow ourselves to love them, then go through the heartbreak of sending them back. My heart could never quite handle the letting go part.

None of the other foster children had ever captured my whole heart like this baby girl. She had the sweetest way of locking her gaze with mine that seemed to wrap around my heart.

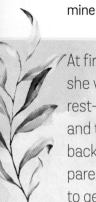

At first I assumed she would be like the rest—stay for a while and then be sent back to live with her parents—so I tried not to get too attached.

We walked the floor with her and made special trips to a local farm for goat's milk. Although she wasn't very content, she became a bright spot in my life. I was a struggling teen trying to find my place and was not very well rooted in the Lord.

At first I assumed she would be like the rest—stay for a while and then be sent back to live with her parents—so I tried not to get too attached. But that didn't last long. I was smitten, and so was the rest of my family.

Time passed. There were at least four occasions when she was almost returned to her family, but then something would happen and the court would rule for her to stay in foster care.

One year . . . Two years . . .

One day the caseworker asked if we would consider adopting her if she came up for adoption. I felt hope rising. Maybe . . . just maybe it could happen. But I refused to consider it as a serious possibility. Trusting these agencies can be difficult. Things are always open to change, and it is easier not to set your heart on anything.

Another year passed.

By this time she was so much a part of our lives that it hurt to even think about her not being there. Although her parents seemed to be out of the picture, we realized her extended family might still want her. And sure enough, her grandparents stepped forward and started the process of having her live with them.

I cannot explain the roller coaster of emotions this put me through. I wanted her to be ours so badly. If you had asked me why, I wouldn't have been able to explain all the reasons, but I really loved this sweet little girl. She would cuddle with me in bed some mornings, her sweetness a beautiful part of my life at a time when things seemed so uncertain.

I begged God to let her stay. *Please don't take her away from us,* my heart pleaded. I was nowhere near a mature Christian, and it felt like my relationship with God hinged on whether He came through for me in this.

I remember how she would cling to my mom and scream when her grandparents came to pick her up for the weekend. They smelled of cigarette smoke and were rough looking, though I think they truly wanted to do what they felt they should for their grandchild. I hated to watch, so I would leave the room, lock myself in the bathroom, and cry. When she came back from her weekend away, it would take her a while to accept love from us again. She had no idea we didn't want her to leave; that we had no choice. To her it felt like rejection.

The day finally came when this beautiful green-eyed girl became my sister. Under the law she was now family; she was here to stay. My parents were her parents. No one could take her from our home.

She was four years old.

My parents named her Lisa to match the rest of us sisters whose names all started with an "L."

She truly is my sister, and the following part is for her:

Lisa, you are such a blessing! I am so thankful you are my sister. When I try to imagine life without you, I cannot.

I thank God that He allowed you to come into our home twenty years ago.

You are no longer that bouncy little girl with pigtails, but a young lady with a life of promise ahead of you.

I pray you will always remember the love that was poured into you, and how grateful we are because of how God uniquely created you for us. You have so much going for you! My prayer is that you will always know you are loved.

God brought you into my life at a crucial time, and He used you to nurture a part of my heart that needed someone little to love. Your presence taught me to love children.

I love spending time with you. In many ways we are alike: we both cry easily, we love animals, and we like to laugh and have a good time. We may have had our disagreements, but you will always have a special place in my heart.

My heart for you is that you will keep pursuing God and all He has for you. With Him, you are never alone. He will never leave you; He will never forsake you.

And remember that I am always here for you.

Through the years, I have met many people who have adopted children or have been adopted. When I think of the wonders of adoption, I think of Romans 8:15: "For ye have not received the spirit of bondage again to fear; but ye have received the Spirit of adoption, whereby we cry, Abba, Father." I love this verse. It so clearly shows how every one of us who names the name of Christ has been adopted into His family as sons and daughters.

God is our Father, and we are His. No matter where you are in life, that is what matters most. Claim the promise of that verse and walk in confidence, knowing that your Father loves you.

My sister's story is beautiful to me. If you have been redeemed, your story is beautiful too.

We are all a part of the family of God. Hallelujah!

CHAPTER NINE

The Eyes of Grief

They that sow in tears shall reap in joy. Psalm 126:5

I saw grief up close today.

Tears filled my eyes as I gazed into the eyes of my cousin, those windows of her soul. I would have done almost anything to take away the deep pain I saw, but I was at a complete loss for words.

They seemed inadequate anyway.

I looked down at the scrapbook in my hands. It was a kind gesture from the many caring people surrounding the family. But compared to the pain, it seemed so small. A once vibrant life had been reduced to memories, cards, pictures, and scrapbook pages.

On the kitchen counter sat a basket with hundreds of sympathy cards. A picture frame stood behind it, bearing an image that was the reason for this aching pain. The beautiful smile on the face remains etched into my mind.

Of course there were no words to say!

My cousin has done one of the hardest things a mother will ever do. She stood by the grave of her twelve-year-old daughter, feeling the sting of death. In a flash of time, she had been thrust onto a pathway no one would ever choose. A day planned with so much excitement had ended in a way no one had dreamed.

A bicycle accident had cut short her daughter's life.

Standing in this mother's kitchen, I was overwhelmed with a feeling so strong I couldn't speak. I realized our lives are like a thread. Each day is a gift.

Oh, I know that every day—yes, everything in my life—must be given to God. But do I really?

The children God has given me are not my own—they are His. I cannot hold tightly to anyone or anything other than Jesus. A hammer and chisel could not have pounded these points home any harder than I felt them now.

Yet I still need to be reminded of these things many times. Oh, I know that every day—yes, everything in my life— must be given to God. But do I really?

I think of how often I become distracted with duties. There is so much to do. I must get my work done, right?

But not at the expense of my family!

I feel a sense of shame for the times I have snapped at my children because I was determined to get my list finished for the day.

As I look at my cousin's family and see the gaping hole in their home, I wonder how I could ever again get so distracted that I forget

in the laundry basket."

Sometimes I get a little weary of the constant mess, but then I am reminded of the saying, "Lord, thank you for the mess in my home. It means I have been blessed." All too soon (older folks tell me) my house will stay the way I cleaned it. All too soon there won't be toys and shoes, coats and Legos scattered about. If I cannot learn to be happy with my life right now, will I be happy in the future?

Probably not.

As I think about cleaning, my mind goes to another place needing regular cleaning. Just as easily as clutter fills our natural house, so can sin and wrong feelings slip into our heart. It takes continual effort to keep my heart pure. If I let things go too long, it is more difficult to get the corners of my heart clean, because those things become habits.

My heart needs the light of truth. In 1 John 2:9-11 we read, "He that saith he is in the light, and hateth his brother, is in darkness even until now. He that loveth his brother abideth in the light, and there is none occasion of stumbling in him. But he that hateth his brother is in darkness, and walketh in darkness, and knoweth not whither he goeth, because that darkness hath blinded his eyes."

> Allowing God's light to shine in my heart exposes the wrong feelings that must be cleaned out.

It is a continual challenge to keep wrong feelings from cluttering my heart. People say or do things that hurt, and then we can easily do the same in return. What I do with my hurt feelings makes all the difference. Allowing God's light to shine in my heart exposes the wrong feelings that must be cleaned out.

I was chatting with a mother recently and she told me how God was teaching her a very basic truth—everything she does must be done in love. Getting a drink for a child, picking up things, packing lunches, even disciplining—unless done in love, "profiteth me nothing." That may seem elementary for a Christian, but it is a foundational truth. And who gives me the ability to love when I don't feel like it? Only God can do that.

If I don't do things in love, my heart will be filled with frustration, bitterness, and wrong attitudes. That is Satan's favorite tactic. He laces our days with discontentment and fills our hearts with annoyance instead of patience and love. Operating on our own strength, our first reaction will not be love.

There is a verse I often pray—Psalm 51:10: "Create in me a clean heart, O God; and renew a right spirit within me." *A clean heart and a right spirit.* If I am open to God and sensitive to His Spirit, He can show me areas of my heart that are not clean. As He declutters those areas, there will be room for His love to fill my heart.

Proverbs 20:7 says, "The just man walketh in his integrity: his children are blessed after him." If I keep my heart clean, it will not only be a blessing for me but also for my children. How much easier to live with a mother who recognizes her weaknesses and admits she was wrong than with a mother who thinks acknowledging wrong is a weakness!

As I take my garbage bag, dust rag, and broom, heading into the next area of my home, my thoughts form a prayer: *Lord, clean out the corners of my heart. Show me how I can better serve you.*

Only by the grace of God can I have a clean heart.

CHAPTER ELEVEN

A Leafy Perspective

Heaviness in the heart of man maketh it stoop:
but a good word maketh it glad. Proverbs 12:25

*L*iving in an area surrounded by trees has its benefits. I love our private setting. My parents' house is the only house we can see from our home. In the summertime when the leaves are on the trees, we can hardly see even that. If my laundry doesn't make its way to the wash line by 10 a.m., no one will ever know. Neither will they know if I leave it out overnight.

There are other benefits to living in the woods. With many in our family being hunters, it's a blessing to have hunting ground right out the back door. We also enjoy the coolness of the shade trees in summer. And in the fall, while other areas have frost, the trees protect our garden and yard.

Wildlife is another positive. We love the many birds merrily chirping away, flocking to our feeders in the winter. We see squirrels and deer, and have seen a bobcat, coyotes, and even bears on our trail camera close to the house.

Yes, we love where God has placed us.

But there are a few negatives. One is the limited view of sunrises and sunsets; the trees block my view. Another drawback is a lack of sunshine on our garden, limiting what we can grow.

One of the biggest negatives for me comes in autumn, when the trees shed their leaves. They pile knee-deep in corner flowerbeds, in the dog runs, against the house, and on my patios. We have leaves everywhere! And if it gets windy, they can't really blow away; they just blow somewhere else. We use the bagger on the mower to collect as many as we can, but it still takes work to get them out of the flowerbeds and corners.

This summer and fall we had so much rain that the leaves didn't change color as quickly as usual. They also stayed on the trees much longer. To top it off, when they finally started to turn, we had a surprise nine inches of snow. Suddenly all the trees seemed to sigh and drop their leaves.

When the snow disappeared, the yard was covered with soggy brown leaves that weren't going to move without help.

Right in the middle of this, I had invited a group of ladies to my house for tea, lunch, and a fun time of chatting. I considered doing some leaf cleanup beforehand, but I just didn't have time. My friends arrived, and soon we were chatting away.

One of the women looked out the window and said, "I just love your place! You have such a nice setting."

I looked out the window where she was standing, and guess what caught my eye? All the leaves! "I do like our place," I said, "but look at all those leaves!"

Another lady stepped over. With a huge smile, she said, "Oh, but I love the leaves! Don't clean them up. I just love the way it looks when the yard is covered with leaves! They are God's decorations."

I glanced back out the window. *Hmmm…* I had never looked at the leaves that way, and the comment stuck with me. Those leaves had always annoyed me. They represented so much work, but now I was seeing them through different eyes.

What I saw negatively, my friend saw as beauty. That can be true of many things in life. It's all a matter of perspective.

Depending on your personality, you might find yourself viewing life through a negative filter. Or perhaps you know someone like that. People who say or think things like, *I just knew it was going to happen. Nothing good ever happens to me. It's probably going to rain. We shouldn't even bother.* It can become a habit to look at a situation and immediately see the negative side.

We understand how absurd it would be to look at a stormy sky and see only the storm clouds instead of the rainbow! Or to see a bright red sky in the morning and get annoyed because it will probably rain soon. How sad if we would sit by a warm fire and say, "Yes, this feels good. But if it wouldn't be so cold, we wouldn't need it!"

Negativity can so quickly change a lovely day into a sour one.

We may not be that drastic, but what happens if someone starts talking about a struggle a certain person is going through? Do we focus on the negative and discuss this person's weaknesses, or do we look for something positive to say? This is a challenge for me! I want to look for the positives in people. Every person is worth the effort it takes to defend and encourage.

Something I have noticed in my home is if Mother is not happy, then most likely no one else in the house is happy either. If I focus on the negatives: *This is dirty. That is broken. This child does this. That child does that. Hubby's not measuring up. The house needs work. My friends don't reach out to me. Nobody cares* . . . Pretty soon I see the same attitude in my children. They have their own versions: *School is ridiculous. The teacher isn't fair. I do all the work around here. My chores aren't fair.*

But just as negativity breeds arguments and sour faces, so positivity is also contagious. It makes for an atmosphere of "I am loved and I want to please."

I know myself. I can flip between positive and negative so quickly. I can start the day positively, but after a couple of knocks I will be looking at things negatively. It takes a constant awareness of my attitude—and a willingness to reevaluate—as I walk through the day.

Sometimes I am so positive with ideas that I launch off into something before I really think it through. At those times I can be really enthusiastic. But sometimes I see only the work and become discouraged. That is often the case when I look inward.

A friend and I did a little research about being positive and found some beautiful Bible verses. One is Proverbs 12:25: "Heaviness in the heart of man maketh it stoop: but a good word maketh it glad." That couldn't be any clearer. Negativity makes our hearts stoop, but a good word or a positive focus makes us glad.

Here's another, my favorite. I think I will post it in bold print on my refrigerator where I can see it every day. It's Isaiah 50:4: "The Lord GOD hath given me the tongue of the learned, that I should know how to speak a word in season to him that is weary."

It is not always easy to live positively. But if our mind is sound, we can learn what it takes to help ourselves focus on the good. Does singing help? Then sing, my friend! Is it sending cards to someone or making a daily list of things to be thankful for? Then do it!

If we sit back and allow ourselves to be negative, Satan has us right where he wants us—incapable of being a benefit to the kingdom. I think again of the words of Isaiah 61:3: "To appoint unto them that mourn in Zion, to give unto them . . . the garment of praise for the spirit of heaviness."

If I focus on the negatives—the work the leaves make, the failures in my life, or the things I wish would be different—I will develop a spirit of heaviness. But with the help of God, I'll enjoy the leaves and robe myself in the garment of praise.

Ready to join me, my friend? We'll sit and enjoy the beauty of the leaves in my yard.

Maybe I'll even hand you a rake and we'll get to work!

CHAPTER TWELVE

Alone on the Street

What? know ye not that your body is the temple of the Holy Ghost which is in you, which ye have of God, and ye are not your own? For ye are bought with a price: therefore glorify God in your body, and in your spirit, which are God's. 1 Corinthians 6:19–20

Uncertain—and a little annoyed—my sister tapped the horn. *Beep!*

Nothing. The car in front of her did not move, though the light had been green for a few seconds.

Whatever! she thought, pushing the horn again. Her teenage mind grew agitated at what seemed like someone not paying attention.

Still nothing. Soon the light changed back to red. "Come on!" she muttered in irritation.

It was early in the morning and few people were around. My sister looked from side to side and tried to peer into the vehicle ahead to see what was causing the problem, wondering what to do. Then the light turned green again.

Now, she thought. But the vehicle in front of her stayed right where it was. After a few long seconds, she decided to drive around it. Pulling up beside the car, she glanced over to see what was going on. By the position of the driver, she sensed he needed help. She tried getting his attention, but he didn't move.

Now with deep concern for the driver, she put her vehicle in park and got out, not worried about her own safety. She tapped on the window of the car. "Are you okay?" she asked loudly. He didn't respond.

She asked again and thought she heard him say something before he went rigid and started with what looked like a seizure.

Oh, no! My sister's mind kicked into overdrive. Feeling completely helpless, she panicked and started yelling for help. Glancing around frantically, she saw people coming at a run. How thankful she was that though it was early in the morning, some other people were on the streets of Ephrata.

Someone called 911. Among those gathered around came fearful exclamations, "He's not breathing! Does anyone know CPR?!" They tried to help him, but it soon became apparent he was not doing well at all.

My sister, as young as she was, knew the signs of death. She had worked in an animal clinic and had seen many an animal take a last breath.

"He's dying!" she yelled, crying desperately. An older woman pulled her away to help her calm down until medical help arrived.

And she was right. He *was* dying. Right there on the street that young man drew his last breath. The medical professionals affirmed it later. He was gone.

Was he sick? Not with a typical disease, but one that can mysteriously afflict a person.

He had overdosed. The drugs in his system had taken his life. The police and the ambulance people knew him. They knew he had a drug problem; he had needed help before. But now it would never happen again. His life, so full of potential and promise, was over.

As you can imagine, it took some time for my sister to work through this incident. It seemed so senseless. Why would someone willingly take a drug that could stop his heart and take his life?

We have all heard of drug overdoses. Our hearts break for those caught in the bondage of a drug addiction and for their families. It turns a beautiful life full of promise and hope into a life of hopelessness and defeat. The person is either looking for a way out or simply just the next fix. The cycle is continuous and deeply painful. When it ends in total defeat and death, we struggle to wrap our minds around how this could be!

Too often we Christians shake our heads and keep our distance. Our attitude can be one of condescension for someone so obviously weak. How can a life become so out of control? Why would anyone choose this?

But wait a minute and think about this with me.

How can we judge a drug, alcohol, or nicotine addiction as worse than other addictions? What about our addiction to food? Or gossip and slander? The addiction to money? Impurity? What about the addiction/idol of being in control or needing to control everyone around us? The list could go on.

The addiction to food is one every one of us can relate to in some form. Why do we eat those foods that have no value but are pleasing to the tongue? The results of overindulging in food are evident, yet we have decided this addiction is acceptable. The Bible speaks against gluttony, but we tend to gloss over it because so many of us struggle with it. But is this any less an addiction than mind-altering drugs?

Overeating is actually a very dangerous addiction. Many of the reasons for joint replacements, as well as heart and lung issues, are closely related to obesity. The medical field is full of stories of people unable to help themselves because they are so overweight. Our bodies are not meant to carry so much extra weight, and the effects are dangerous—it can literally take your life. It may not be as drastic as a heroin overdose, but eventually it will cause problems that can result in death.

As an addiction, eating can consume our thoughts. We think about what we will eat next, or if we're trying not to eat so much, we can become obsessed with not eating. Either way, food becomes a distraction and takes our focus off Christ, right where Satan would have us. We go to food for comfort in times of stress instead of to the Lord. Is this any less serious than the drug epidemic? God has convicted me to be careful not to allow food to become my focus. Controlling this addiction has not been easy.

It is the same with being addicted to gossip. We women need to be careful with this because we are so relational. Our lives center around people, and we can easily take

> My body, including everything I put into it or allow myself to indulge in, needs to align with God and His will for my life.

delight in hearing about other people's failures or problems, somehow thinking it lessens our own. If we pass these stories along to others, we are feeding the addiction. The pull grows stronger for the next "good story."

This may not take our physical lives, but our spiritual life is sure to suffer. The worst effects of this addiction are the wounded souls who have been hurt by lies, slander, and gossip. There are deep, deep wounds that come from being judged or talked about negatively. I have been guilty of not stopping something I knew should not be discussed. I have also shared things I shouldn't have. Am I alarmed by this addiction? I should be!

I have done a lot of soul searching about addictions. The following comes to mind: "What? know ye not that your body is the temple of the Holy Ghost which is in you, which ye have of God, and ye are not your own? For ye are bought with a price: therefore glorify God in your body, and in your spirit, which are God's" (1 Corinthians 6:19–20). These verses have become precious to me as I have tried to deal with some idols I have allowed in my life.

I am not my own; I am the Lord's. He has paid the highest price imaginable so I could come to Him. My body, including everything I put into it or allow myself to indulge in, needs to align with God and His will for my life.

It must be a lifestyle choice. My dependence needs to be on God and God alone. I would never take a syringe and fill my veins with drugs to separate myself from reality or hide my pain. But am I free from other addictions? If I search my heart, I see I am no better than the young man whose life was snuffed out by drugs. But for the grace of God, that could have been me.

I must remember that nothing on this earth can ever satisfy or fill that God–vacancy in the depth of my soul. Not drugs, not fun times, not any person or thing, not food, not laughter, not pretense.

Only God can truly satisfy and be all that I need.

CHAPTER THIRTEEN

Battle of the Flea

Cleanse thou me from secret faults. Psalm 19:12

I was terribly disturbed.

Was that a flea I just saw? On my arm?!

Ugh!

In the valley where we live, we have a problem with local people dropping off cats or kittens when they don't want them. Stray cats often carry fleas, and it creates a constant battle with these nasty little bugs on our dogs. We had noticed some again but just hadn't gotten anywhere for treatment supplies. And a few fleas can multiply so fast they become a colony of thousands in short order.

I had heard of people having fleas in their houses. That always made me shudder! I hate bugs! And thinking of having these ugly jumping things in my house . . . Well, you can imagine how I was feeling!

I wasn't positive it was a flea I had seen, but my mind started whirling. Off came the blankets on the sofas and chairs, out went the rugs, down came the bedding from all the beds. I washed things in hot water all that day and the next. We suspected fleas with any bites we saw on ourselves, even though it was summer and mosquitoes abounded.

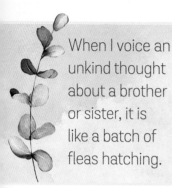

When I voice an unkind thought about a brother or sister, it is like a batch of fleas hatching.

You may think I overreacted. I mean, really, we didn't KNOW we had them in the house. But that's how your imagination can work. If you believe something is there, you suddenly see it everywhere. I was taking no chances!

We spent a lot of time and money treating the dogs and their pens. *If only I had been more urgent when we first noticed them*, I kept thinking. *Then the problem wouldn't be so big.* Getting ahead of the flea cycle takes time and diligence. It is much better to be proactive than reactive.

Fleas love dark corners and hidden places. A flea can live up to a hundred days without a blood supply. The key is to kill the eggs so they can no longer multiply and then treat to get rid of the adults. A few weeks after the first round of treatment, you have to do it again to make sure you get every single one. If you allow them to lay eggs, you will be right back where you started!

If a dog is not taken care of, the damage fleas can do is very painful. The dog goes nearly mad with the ferocity of the itching, even losing hair in places. The fleas can make large, irritated spots on the skin.

Those nasty fleas are an example of how Satan can subtly tempt us with sin. Maybe it starts as an annoyance. As we let our mind dwell on that, it grows, and we can easily judge a person unfairly. We may give in to gossip, passing our opinion on to others. Slowly, subtly, the infestation grows. Before we realize it, we have caused a lot of damage with our judgmental thinking.

We need God's protection to guard us from the temptation to become judgmental in our thoughts and actions. When I voice an unkind thought about a brother or sister, it is like a batch of fleas hatching. It is much harder to fix things after we have been vocal about something.

James 1:13–16 adds to this thought: "Let no man say when he is tempted, I am tempted of God: for God cannot be tempted with evil, neither tempteth he any man. But every man is tempted, when he is drawn away of his own lust, and enticed. Then when lust hath conceived, it bringeth forth sin: and sin, when it is finished, bringeth forth death. Do not err, my beloved brethren."

If you have ever been the victim of unfair judgment, you know the pain it brings. I need God's wisdom to attack negative thoughts with the same intensity I attacked those fleas.

CHAPTER FOURTEEN

Peace . . . With a Sign

Peace I leave with you, my peace I give unto you: not as the world giveth, give I unto you. Let not your heart be troubled, neither let it be afraid. John 14:27

My heart was in turmoil.

We had spent a few weeks agonizing over a decision. Once we decided what we needed to do, we knew our decision was going to cause friction.

Conflict makes my stomach hurt. But as an adult, I realize conflict is a part of life. Situations will arise, decisions need to be made, and conflicts happen.

This situation was touchy from the start. If we chose one side, some people would be happy and others disappointed. The same was true in reverse. Either way we would disappoint someone. Decisions like this cause me much anxiety because I am a people-pleaser.

Our children were very much on one side, adding to my anxiety.

The decision we chose was not their choice, and they did not understand our thinking. We did what we felt God wanted us to do, but my fears proved true—we disappointed some people and caused some negative emotions.

Questioning our decision, I got ready for church that Sunday morning. Fighting tears, I prayed, *Lord, help me know what we have chosen is right. Are you satisfied with our decision? Could you please help me know it will be okay?*

I desperately wanted reassurance that God was pleased with our decision. I breathed a prayer to calm myself. I have learned prayer works better than anything else to ease a troubled heart.

> Understanding that God is in total control brings a peace that can make all things right in our world.

It wasn't a very happy family that headed out the door to church. Our children were disappointed because they wanted "the other choice." Some were quiet and the older ones were a little sullen. The little ones, sensing something was amiss, seemed extra irritable.

My husband and I were also quiet.

"Are you sure we did the right thing?" I asked, my stomach churning. I immediately felt bad. We had made a decision; why question it now? My husband didn't answer, so I knew he felt the same way.

Down the road we went. The morning was beautiful, with the sun's rays peeking through the fog along the tree line. We came to the stop sign at the end of our quiet road and made a left turn toward church. Seeing that a vehicle had slowed down ahead of us, we looked to see what had caught their attention.

And there was my sign.

Standing along the tree line, a ray of sunlight shining directly on her, was a beautiful white deer. Head erect, she looked directly at us—ears forward, her body perfectly still.

It took my breath away.

Adding to the wonder, she suddenly ducked her head. Then, lifting it again, she daintily took a few steps toward us, never taking her eyes off our vehicle.

With a background of fog and the sun shining on her, it almost looked like a mirage—a figment of our imagination. I had never seen a white deer in the wild. What a beautiful creature!

A warm feeling flooded through me. *Thank you, Jesus,* I whispered. Seeing more cars coming behind us, we continued on to church. The children chattered excitedly about what we had seen, but I felt tears fill my eyes.

What a beautiful moment!

God had put her there just for us! Both my husband and I enjoy wildlife immensely. God knew what would get our attention. I don't believe in coincidence. That white deer, standing there at just the right time, was to us the touch of God.

All through church that morning, I experienced a feeling of awe and peace. God placed such calmness within my heart that I no longer questioned our decision. It was right.

I thought of a line I had always enjoyed in the book *Anne of Green Gables.* "God is in His heaven, and all is right with the world." That line has always intrigued me. Understanding that God is in total control brings a peace that can make all things right in our world.

Even when we grapple with circumstances and struggle to be

confident in a choice we have made, we can rest in the fact that God is in control. Not because everything always works out perfectly or God gives us a sign like a beautiful white deer. But because we know and trust that our lives are in His hands.

We never saw the white deer again, but others in the neighborhood said they saw her around the fields and woods close by. She certainly was a beautiful rarity. After hunting season, she was gone.

I will always remember her standing in the field that morning. The peace that flooded my heart strengthened my faith. God loves us that way. He knows just what it will take to show us His special favor. If He chooses, He can bring peace . . . with a sign.

CHAPTER FIFTEEN

Holding the Line

And he said unto me, My grace is sufficient for thee: for my strength is made perfect in weakness. 2 Corinthians 12:9

"Don't you just get tired of it?" The question made me pause. *Get tired of it? What does she mean?*

"To be honest, no," I finally replied. The woman was asking me about maintaining a consistent, healthy weight when unhealthy choices come at us from every direction. And she was tired of it.

Maybe when I first came face to face with my food weaknesses, yes, I did get tired of it. The battle to change the negative ruts in my mind was a difficult one. It was easy to become overwhelmed and, well, just tired of it.

But as I think about this question, I realize this kind of thinking is the root of the problem. For lots of things, actually.

Do you get tired of loving your children? Your husband? Your friends? Sure, some days you need to dig a little deeper to show love, but we don't spend a lot of time thinking about getting tired of it. Why?

Because in our minds we have already made a choice. And so, day after day, time after time, choice after choice, we love.

> Life is all about choices. When I make my choice for God, it needs to change my life.

Do we get tired of loving Jesus? Of serving God? Do we get tired of the Bible? Of going to church? Maybe so, but we struggle to get back on track. We pray and cry and seek. Why?

Because we have made a choice to serve God. We long to be with Him. We want heaven. We want peace and everlasting life.

I just had a talk with my son about choices. He's impulsive (like his mother) and sometimes he suffers the consequences of a wrong choice. But this week he made the right choice, and I am praying the good feelings from that right choice will help him make many more good choices.

I'm sure you've heard the saying, "I will do what I want to do." That is so true.

This inward determination is what helps us make healthy food choices. It is also what helps us be faithful to our spouses. To be dedicated mothers, devoted church attendees, faithful Bible readers, and faithful followers of the Father who calls us to Himself.

Drawing that line in my mind will help me pause at gossip, choose kindness over sarcasm, give others the benefit of the doubt, and be gentle and compassionate instead of opinionated and quarrelsome.

If I live with the open option of, "I just might get tired of this when push comes to shove," we cannot succeed in life. We will be too lazy to make healthy choices.

I'm not talking about positive thinking or just plain determination. I am talking about a deep-down heart and soul choice.

How could the Apostle Paul say in Philippians 4:11, "For I have learned, in whatsoever state I am, therewith to be content"? It was because he had made a choice. He was choosing to be content, no matter where God placed him or what he had to face.

Life is all about choices. When I make my choice for God, it needs to change my life. It dare not be a haphazard, I'll-do-this-until-I-am-tired-of-it choice, but a commitment, no matter what.

So the answer is no. I do not get tired of it. I will not allow myself to think I am tired of choosing fruit over whoopie pies any more than I am tired of disciplining my children God's way.

I will draw a line.

In 2 Corinthians 12:9 we find God's promise for those who are weak: "And he said unto me, My grace is sufficient for thee: for my strength is made perfect in weakness. Most gladly therefore will I rather glory in my infirmities, that the power of Christ may rest upon me." In my weakness I can call on a God who understands and is able to give me the strength to hold that line firmly.

I'm not tired of it.

By God's grace, I am holding the line.

CHAPTER SIXTEEN

Let's Be Friends

*And Ruth said, Intreat me not to leave thee, or to return from following
after thee: for whither thou goest, I will go; and where thou lodgest, I will
lodge: thy people shall be my people, and thy God my God.* Ruth 1:16

Church was extremely full.

I sat down at the end of the bench and watched as the ushers tried to find room for everyone. A row of young ladies filed in and set up chairs down the middle aisle. One unfolded her chair and sat down beside me.

I glanced over at her, ready to give the ordinary, friendly greeting. Our eyes connected, and I noticed a sparkle in hers that drew me. We exchanged a short, friendly greeting. She told me her name and who she was. Being Mennonite, and doing what we do, I soon realized I knew some of her extended family and could make connections with her.

A smile lit up her face. Something about her intrigued me. She was a beautiful young woman, full of life and enthusiasm. She had a wide, sweet smile for a stranger—even a middle-aged mom like me. I sensed we could be kindred spirits, but with the age difference and the distance between home locations, I never thought there would be any further connection.

Fast forward a year or so.

I am sitting at my kitchen table with this same young lady. It is amazing how God works! She is a niece to a friend who has come to visit me.

As the three of us sip lattes and chat, I think back to the first time I met her. I'm intrigued that I now count her as a friend. Many things had to take place in both of our lives to bring about this connection.

I marvel at how God works to bring about such connections, often leading to a friendship that is an asset to everyone involved. I am blessed with quite a few God-connection friendships, and I treasure each one.

We can easily miss out on a potential friendship by being too self-focused. I recently talked with a woman who told me she has no close friends. "I'm just not a friendly person, I guess," she added rather flippantly. But I could sense that under those words lay a world of hurt.

I cannot imagine life without friends.

We need each other. God has blessed us with the ability to connect with and encourage each other—in ways nothing else in His creation is able to do. We also have the potential to hurt each other's hearts as no other creature can. And a wounded heart struggles to connect with others to make friends. This tightly closed and protected heart will not allow anyone to get too close.

Friendships can be forged between different ages and from anywhere. Too often we put up boundaries and miss beautiful connections. In the Bible is the story of how Ruth became friends with her mother-in-law Naomi and how they looked out for each other in beautiful ways.

> True friendship allows for honesty, open dialogue, and being vulnerable enough to hear the truth spoken in love.

Sometimes friendships form almost instantly. Have you ever met someone you knew immediately was going to be a good friend? David and Jonathan were like that. "And it came to pass, when he had made an end of speaking unto Saul, that the soul of Jonathan was knit with the soul of David, and Jonathan loved him as his own soul" (1 Samuel 18:1).

Jesus' friendship with Mary, Martha, and Lazarus was close enough that it was safe to be vulnerable to each other. True friends share openly, whether right or wrong. They tell each other the truth and help each other toward Christ. Let's look at the conversation between Martha and Jesus in John 11:21–23: "Then said Martha unto Jesus, Lord, if thou hadst been here, my brother had not died. But I know, that even now, whatsoever thou wilt ask of God, God will give it thee. Jesus saith unto her, Thy brother shall rise again."

This interaction shows an open, honest friendship. Martha shared her disappointment and sadness with Jesus, and He showed her the truth. True friendship allows for honesty, open dialogue, and being vulnerable enough to hear the truth spoken in love.

I thank God for every one of my friends. But most of all, I want to be a friend of God. The Bible says Abraham was God's friend. They had a relationship of respect and obedience. When God spoke, Abraham immediately obeyed. He trusted God to lead him where he was supposed to go.

As I nurture the friendships God has given me, the only way to be a true friend is to prioritize a deep friendship with my heavenly Father. My earthly friendships will then be blessed in the ways that matter most.

Come. Sip a latte with me, my friends. Let's share our hearts and seek our Father.

Together.

CHAPTER SEVENTEEN

All Fear Gone

*For God hath not given us the spirit of fear; but of power,
and of love, and of a sound mind.* 2 Timothy 1:7

When I was young, I had a severe phobia of heights. Whether I was coming down the ladder from the haymow or climbing the rope swing over the creek in our meadow, a debilitating fear would grip my heart, making me light-headed and trembly from the inside out. I just couldn't do it!

If you have a fear of heights, you know what I mean. It is a heart-pounding, weak-kneed feeling that turns your muscles to jelly and the rest of your body into a rigid mass of stubborn immobility. Even a picture can give me these symptoms, depending on the angle—a high walkway, a balcony, an overhanging rock. Just the thought of falling over the edge causes a reaction for me.

A few years ago we went to Tennessee for a family vacation. The higher we drove along the mountain roads, the more agitated I felt. Occasionally I would suck in my breath and remind my husband to "stay over," horrified by the absence of guardrails. I thought there should be a block wall about eight feet high! The children laughed at me in amazement, wondering why I was so afraid.

How could I explain? I knew my husband would do his best to stay on the road, but no matter how much I believed it in my mind, the rest of me would not behave.

I have always had that fear. My mind goes back to the days of pigtails and barefoot summers. I remember standing near the edge of the ladder descending from the haymow, trying to talk myself into going down. My brothers and sisters would grab hold of the edge of the hole and, facing forward, just step down the ladder. My mouth would go dry and I could not move. No matter how much I wanted to, I could not make myself step into that abyss. My way of approaching the ladder was to get down on my knees, back up, and shakily drop one foot until it rested firmly on a stable rung. Even then, I could barely breathe until I set my feet once again on the solid concrete down below.

Since those days I have braved many heights. I was at the top of the World Trade Center several years before the two towers were destroyed, and later I braved the Freedom Tower. I drove over the Chesapeake Bay Bridge in Maryland, I flew in an airplane on a two-week mission trip to Canada, I looked out the top of the arch at the Gateway to the West in St. Louis, and I took a cog train up Mt. Washington. And yes, every single time I fought both my body and my mind as my adrenal glands went haywire.

Why would I do things that make my heart pound wildly and cause dizziness in my head? Why would I bother to fight the fear? The leaden feet, the bile in my throat, the shaking of my hands and knees? Is it worth it?

Yes!

You see, I will not be defined by my fear. I am also blessed with an adventurous spirit and a genetic stubbornness.

I remember the glory of the sunset as we rose from a rainy, dreary runway up beyond the clouds into the bright hues of the sun. I would never have witnessed such a breathtaking scene had I given way to my fears. I remember the blue mountain ranges spreading miles and miles in all directions from the heights of Clingman's Dome in the Smoky Mountains. And I think of the rush of tears I often experience as I gaze in wonder over a beautiful scene that took all my willpower to approach.

Even writing about these moments brings a shortness of breath and a spike in my heart rate. It is a handicap—one the professionals have labeled "acrophobia." According to Wikipedia, one out of twenty adults suffer from this. It is nice to know I am not alone!

Fear can rob a person of so many beautiful things in life.

Often I have needed to take some moments to calm myself and do "head talk," which usually ends up being a frantic prayer: *God, help me control my breathing. I want to see this. I want to say I have done this!* I have learned (after the disappointment of being too afraid and missing some beautiful things) that by forcing myself to keep going, I can enjoy heights to a certain extent.

So why would I bother to push myself beyond what I think I can handle?

It is simple. As much as I hate the fear, I absolutely love the peak.

This fear reminds me of the way Satan handicaps us in our walk with the Lord. He takes natural things—things that can be frightening—and enlarges them in our minds until the fear becomes bigger than our trust in God.

What if something happens to my husband? What if I get cancer? What if my husband loses his job? What if my children make bad choices?

These debilitating fears cause us to take control and try to manage things on our own, leaving God out of the equation. We tightly control our home, our children, and our husband out of a spirit of fear.

As a young person, we may have had fears of gaining weight, not meeting that perfect someone, or being friendless or rejected. The choices we make outside of God to control those fears can follow us the rest of our lives. These fears can define us as a person if we allow them to control us.

I think of the fear of displeasing people. If we allow that fear to take control, we become a people-pleaser more than a God-pleaser. We soon find ourselves frustrated and maxed out.

In 2 Timothy 1:7 we read, "For God hath not given us the spirit of fear; but of power, and of love, and of a sound mind."

With my hand in my Savior's, I can rise above my fears and view my world through eyes of trust.

Can we find victory over these fears that rob us of peace, sleep, and confidence in the Lord?

Yes!

We can use the same principles to fight our soul-fears as I do my earthly fears. I recognize the fears and do the prayer-talk. God gives me strength to put the fears where they belong—in His hands. It comes down to making a choice. With truth, I can reject Satan's fears and reach the heights of God's peak.

Fear will rob me of more than I can ever imagine. But if I am willing to face it squarely, with my hand in God's, I can have victory. I might always have a weakness for certain fears, but I need not live in bondage to them.

I may suffer from what the world calls acrophobia. I accept that. But there is no way I want to be labeled with acrophobia in God's kingdom. With my hand in my Savior's, I can rise above my fears and view my world through eyes of trust.

I'm confident the heights of heaven will bring pure ecstasy to me—all fear will be completely gone.

I will never be afraid again!

CHAPTER EIGHTEEN

Love ... In a Pair of Shoes

That if thou shalt confess with thy mouth the Lord Jesus,
and shalt believe in thine heart that God hath raised him
from the dead, thou shalt be saved. Romans 10:9

I glanced down at the floor I was washing on my hands and knees. I noticed the spot where the tear had dripped off my chin. It left a small circle of wetness on my yet unwashed floor. I wiped it up as I continued my scrubbing.

I have never tried washing the floor with my tears before, I thought as another tear joined the first.

Minutes before I had been focusing on my cleaning, singing as I worked. Now the tears dripped in a steady rhythm off my chin.

Tears have always been a big part of who I am. They can mean a lot of things. Sometimes they are tears of joy, laughter, or even excitement. My tears can also mean sadness, discouragement, or overwhelming emotions. I have often wished I could turn them off, but only rarely can I do that. They just slip out unbidden.

The tears today were not from anything negative. They came from overwhelmed emotions.

It wasn't a big deal to my friend. A simple text, then a phone call, "Hey, I'm shopping, and there's a really nice pair of shoes on sale!" She described them, knowing I was looking for shoes, and in a few minutes agreed to get me a pair. We hung up. A few sweet words and, just like that, I was getting a new pair of shoes!

I was overwhelmed. Feeling loved, my heart overflowed with gratitude for the kind actions of my friend. Out of my heart and through my eyes came the tears. Tears of thankfulness for a friend who knew me well and cared enough to buy me shoes.

I'm not used to that—and it's my own fault. I have always been very self-sufficient. I hate to ask or be a bother to anyone. I would rather do things for others than have them do things for me. This might not be all bad, but I need to check the underlying attitude.

To my friend, it was just what friends do. That's who she is and always has been. But to me, it was an unexpected touch of kindness. That's what brought tears to my eyes.

Accepting love has never been easy for me. I've always felt like I need to earn it somehow, that I need to do something so I am worth loving. Recently the Lord has been teaching me otherwise. In 2 Timothy 1:9 it says, "Who hath saved us, and called us with an holy calling, *not according to our works*, but according to his own purpose and grace, which was given us in Christ Jesus before the world began" (emphasis mine).

The reality is, I can never be good enough to earn love.

I can never be a good enough wife, mother, or friend. I can certainly never be a good enough child of God. I'd like to be able to make every-one around me happy, and then . . . *then* . . . I can accept their love for me. I have always lived my life this way, desperately trying to do all I can to please those around me—and even my Lord.

God has been working on me in this area. Recently I have faced situations where I cannot please everyone no matter how hard I try. This feels devastating! My people-pleasing nature starts frantically looking for some way to fix this but sees there is nothing I can do. Over and over, I have had to give it to the Lord and let Him handle it.

Today God was showing me once again, through the kindness of a friend, that I am worth loving—and not because of something I had done. I had not done anything for my friend. I was simply myself, full of mistakes and bumbling. Yet she loved me.

How much more does my heavenly Father love me despite my failures?

I was guided to Romans 10:9 during my time with Jesus this morning: "That if thou shalt confess with thy mouth the Lord Jesus, and shalt believe in thine heart that God hath raised him from the dead, thou shalt be saved."

> Keep your heart open. God might come in small ways to do some great work in your life.

Any good I can do or any good I have ever done is only because of Him. I cannot earn His love any more than I can earn a friendship. Sooner or later I will mess up. I will do things wrong and make choices I regret. And yet He loves me.

Salvation is a gift. It is offered with the greatest sacrifice of love possible—Jesus gave His life on the cross to pay for my sins.

I need to accept this gift and learn that I am worthy of love. Not because of who I am or what I have done, but simply because I am HIS. I need only to come to Him and let Him love me. Knowing me, I will have to remind myself of this truth the rest of my life.

Who would think an offer of shoes would help settle such a truth in my heart? But that's how God is. He works in many ways to draw us to Himself.

Keep your heart open. God might come in small ways to do some great work in your life. Just like He showed His love for me today . . . in a pair of shoes.

CHAPTER NINETEEN

Because of a Little Song

*Be kindly affectioned one to another with brotherly love;
in honour preferring one another.* Romans 12:10

Their little faces shone with delight as they sang.

"Away in a manger, no crib for a bed, the little Lord Jesus laid down His sweet head . . ."

I always have trouble keeping tears at bay when I listen to little people sing so sweetly. As I looked from one cheery face to the next, my heart pondered the meaningful words of that beautiful Christmas song we know so well.

Today was our school's Christmas dinner. We always gather before lunch and the students sing a few songs for us. After they sing, we all join our voices in more Christmas songs before eating lunch.

It is a special day. We enjoy spending time together in our little school, and I appreciate our close-knit school community. We have always sent our children to this private school.

As grades 1–4 sang, my heart filled with gratitude for the blessing of knowing the real meaning of Christmas. The last verse of "Away in a Manger" is such a beautiful prayer:

> Be near me, Lord Jesus; I ask Thee to stay
> Close by me forever, and love me, I pray.
> Bless all the dear children in Thy tender care,
> And take us to heaven to live with Thee there.

The teachers had spent a good amount of time with the children to help them learn this song well. I know these little people cannot grasp the full meaning of the words they have worked to memorize, but that prayer is so precious.

As parents, we want the Lord to be near to our children. We know He will always love them, and we want His blessing to rest upon them all their lives—and then throughout eternity.

As their voices sang the final notes of that familiar song, I thought of the beauty of a well-functioning school. Though they are a body of students, each one is unique. Whether they are in the upper or lower grades, they are part of the group, under the authority of a teacher. If each student would decide to do his or her own thing, chaos would reign.

Some school terms don't go so well, and other terms go more smoothly. This is normal in any school. It is a blessing when everyone can work together to make the school term a success. After nine years as school patrons, we have learned we cannot expect this to just happen. We as parents need to be faithfully involved so our children can know we support them and their teacher.

This is also true for a family and a church. It means a lot of give and take, a lot of patience and understanding. And a lot of brotherly love.

We can sit back and pick out the things we don't like about our family, school, or church. Or we can roll up our sleeves and do what we can to make things better, learning to truly pray the serenity prayer: "God, grant me the serenity to accept the things I cannot change, the courage to change the things I can, and the wisdom to know the difference."

We all have the same goal—to one day be in heaven with Jesus.

Not everyone views life the same way. There are different ways to accomplish the same goal. The beauty of Christian brotherhood is laying aside differences and accepting each other the way Jesus calls us to, working together to glorify the Lord in all we do.

Too often we allow petty things to drive a wedge between us. We may exalt our own lifestyle or our way of serving the Lord, looking down on a brother or sister who chooses something different. These attitudes cause a lot of pain among Christians.

As the words of that little song ring in my mind, "... and take us to heaven to live with Thee there," I thank God for the beauty of Christian unity. I am not referring to the way we dress or the way we do this or that. I am referring to like-mindedness in CHRIST.

We all have the same goal—to one day be in heaven with Jesus.

I love to sing like we did today, but one day the heavens will ring with beautiful singing of *all* the saints in worship together.

I want to be there!

On that day, I will sing with my whole heart—and no tears will choke out the words.

CHAPTER TWENTY

Without Eruption

*But be ye doers of the word, and not hearers only,
deceiving your own selves.* James 1:22

*I*t happened nearly forty years ago, the year I was born.
Recently I stumbled across an article on the May 1980 eruption of Mount St. Helens. The old National Geographic I found in my closet pictured a huge plume of smoke and ash that reached a height of almost twelve miles. I found the facts morbidly fascinating.

Many warning signs preluded the massive eruption: two months of slight earthquakes, magma seeping over the top of the volcano, a minor eruption in March, and visible bulges on the mountain's surface. Many scientists were closely monitoring the situation, but they were still unprepared for the big one.

Moments before the blast, David Johnston, a volcanologist on site, radioed the USGS base to warn them that the big one was imminent. He lost his life in the eruption.

As I read the article, my mind began to stir.

God's people have many warning signs. The Scriptures warn of many things. Like the people living around Mount St. Helens, we may realize that things are getting worse—not just in the world around us, but in our homes, our churches, our schools, and our families.

People seem increasingly angry and unsympathetic. "Christians" bicker among themselves, unable to settle the smallest disputes. Marriages are in chaos because neither side will lay down their rights. Gossip and slander run rampant until the pain bulges in hurting hearts all over.

We see the signs and shake our heads—but then allow our own hearts to become lax in guarding our souls against Satan's all-out attack.

Many people living around Mount St. Helens prepared themselves when they heard dire predictions. They purchased gas masks and stocked up on groceries, but history books say the preparation and rescue were chaotic and disorganized. They just didn't grasp the magnitude of what could happen.

When a person's thought patterns are not controlled, they lead to eruptions of a different kind.

Eighty-three-year-old Harry R. Truman (not the president) became somewhat of a celebrity during the months leading up to the explosion for his blatant refusal to leave the mountain. He scoffed at public concern for his safety, insisting he would be fine. "You couldn't pull me out with a mule team!" he said, claiming it was all just a bunch of geological hype. His body was never found.

What about us? Can we hear godly counsel even if we're not quite convinced of the danger? We might hear the Word of God preached, and conviction grips our hearts. But unless we are willing to take definite steps to change, we will continue our usual actions, reactions, and sinful patterns. And when a person's thought patterns are not controlled, they lead to eruptions of a different kind.

A mother finds herself red-faced and shouting at her child—again. In the heat of the moment, she ignores the nudges of conviction, and her eruption causes damage to a tender heart. The ash of her anger settles deep into the heart of her child.

A father, losing his temper, punishes his child with too much force. The spanking becomes a beating, and the aftermath of that eruption carries lifelong repercussions. Little hearts—intended to be soft—become hard.

A selfish adult gives in to an eruption of uncontrolled lust and sexually preys on the innocence of a child. The damage is catastrophic.

A rumor erupts and flows from person to person until someone's dignity lies trampled at the feet of condescending "concerned" Christians. And another soul falls victim to despondency and depression.

Eruptions like this are happening all around us!

What can we do to make sure we are not among the guilty ones? James 1:22 says, "But be ye doers of the word, and not hearers only, deceiving your own selves." If God is convicting your heart of sinful tendencies, take heed before an eruption disfigures your life and that of someone else.

One heart damaged by a careless eruption is one heart too many. I need to hear the Word and be a doer. I need to take the truths in

God's Word and live them out with the help of my Father.

The last paragraph of the National Geographic article really stirred my heart: "Science helps us understand many things: we can track a hurricane and measure a tsunami's wall of water. But some things are beyond the dissecting lens of science. An aching heart, for one."

That's right, who can measure the ache in a heart? Or realize the wounds of the abused? Who can truly understand the pain of a soul who is misunderstood or damaged by slander and careless words?

I know of only one Source who is able to handle the hurts that come because of sinful eruptions. "Come unto me," He says, "all ye that labour and are heavy laden, and I will give you rest" (Matthew 11:28).

May we walk close to God so we will never be the ones to cause such hurts. "Lord, help me walk faithfully. When I feel things building in my life that could cause sinful eruptions, convict me before it is too late. Help me see myself for who I really am."

How is the pressure inside you?

God is ready and willing to release it for you—without an eruption.

CHAPTER TWENTY-ONE

Two-Minute Rainbow

For he hath said, I will never leave thee, nor forsake thee. Hebrews 13:5

"Mommy, look! A rainbow!"

I slowed the vehicle to a stop at the end of the driveway and looked up. Sure enough, straight in front of me was a beautiful, bright rainbow, right in the middle of the small section of sky visible above the trees.

Putting the vehicle into park, I jumped out to take a picture.

I love rainbows, but I hadn't seen one for a long time. Because we live in the woods, our view of the sky is limited, especially in the summer.

In awe, I snapped a few pictures, then got back into my vehicle. I was so thankful that my daughter had noticed it. I started down the road to more open sky, hoping to see it better. But to my surprise, it was gone. Had my little girl not pointed it out, I would have completely missed it. So quickly it was there and then gone . . .

I felt a thrill go through me. Knowing I had nearly missed it made it feel like my own personal rainbow. A special gift from God.

Just for me.

I needed that today. I was walking through a day of sadness, dealing with a relationship that was hard to understand. I had been longing for a personal touch from God, though I hadn't asked for it—and I certainly hadn't thought of a rainbow.

> The only way to live in freedom is to keep our focus on things above.

But I didn't have to; He saw my heart. He understood the aching in my soul. He knew I needed a reminder of His love. His promise.

I thought of the ending of Hebrews 13:5: "For he hath said, I will never leave thee, nor forsake thee." I felt His presence in such a personal way—that sweet God-touch wrapping His love around me.

So often during an intense time we forget to look up. We find it difficult to separate the distractions of normal living from the distractions Satan is throwing at us. He wants to keep our focus from what really matters—from walking hand in hand with our Father.

We forget there is a spiritual battle going on between the forces of good and the forces of evil. Satan wants us distracted, unfocused, and battle weary, so we shuffle along, eyes downcast.

The only way to live in freedom is to keep our focus on things above.

We simply need to look up. A whisper of His name. A kind word. A rainbow. Each can be used by God to say, "My child . . . I'm here. Look up."

That two-minute rainbow was just what I needed. God's promises are sure, no matter what life brings my way.

He will never fail.

CHAPTER TWENTY-TWO

100% Committed

But godliness with contentment is great gain. 1 Timothy 6:6

*I*f someone asks what I think, it makes me cringe.

To be honest, sometimes it takes me a while to know what I actually "think" about a certain thing; I need to mull it over for a bit.

That's what happened the day we went to visit a Hutterite colony.

My cousin and her family invited us to go with them for an evening at a Hutterite colony in Montana. Though I had not given it much thought, I had often wished to experience the way the Hutterite people live.

I was fascinated. Laura, the young Hutterite woman who showed us around the colony, was very friendly. Her beautiful smile lit up her face, and the twinkle in her eyes showed she enjoyed having us there.

The tour was intriguing. After visiting for a while in her house, which was identical to all the other houses on the outside, she showed us the colony's laundry room, the huge kitchen with commercial appliances, and the community dining room where everyone gathered for meals. We toured the attached meetinghouse where services were held each evening.

As we walked along, Laura explained how things work. Everyone has a job, and everyone does their part, all for the good of the colony. If this is your week to peel potatoes, then you peel potatoes. If it's your week to wash dishes, that's what you do. No one prospers on their own but all work together as a whole. She talked of the dairy barn, the eleven-acre garden, the mechanic shop, and the chicken houses. The colony was proud to be self-sufficient and financially successful.

The place was meticulously clean, with spotless floors and appliances. But as she explained how the adults and the children were separated, both in the community dining room and the daily church services, I could barely fathom the lack of family time. It was hard to imagine living without the spontaneity and interruptions children bring.

After our tour, Laura invited us back to her house for a dessert. With her modest garb, she was so hospitable and kind, offering tea and coffee and no-bake cheesecake. I watched, fascinated, as Hutterite women came and went without invitation or Laura even acknowledging them. These women wanted to see the visitors, so they just came right in to have a look—no knocking needed.

I loved Laura's clipped German accent and tried to quiet my children's giggles at some of the strange ways she pronounced common English words. We laughed together as we discussed the different ways to say the same word in German and Pennsylvania Dutch.

Before we had arrived, my cousin had told me, "After we leave, I'd like to hear what you think. I know you are a writer, so I'd love for you to write about this." So as we walked, talked, and experienced an evening with the Hutterites, my writer's eye was alert.

One of my first thoughts as I listened and witnessed their rigid way of life (especially for the women) was, "Thank you, Lord, that I was not born a Hutterite." But then I thought of others who may say the same thing about Mennonites or Amish and decided that wasn't an appropriate prayer.

I asked Laura at one point if she was happy here in this culture. I smiled at her answer. "Oh, fifty-fifty," she said, shrugging her shoulders. "Most times I am. But sometimes I wonder what another life would be like."

That sparked a train of thought.

Am I happy where I am? Is my choice of religion or culture a fifty-fifty choice?

Laura meant the culture—the way of life as a Hutterite—but I took it a step further. Am I fifty-fifty committed to the Lord, or am I in it 100 percent? What about my church? Is it simply a fifty-fifty thing or am I 100 percent committed?

God warned the church of the Laodiceans: "These things saith the Amen, the faithful and true witness, the beginning of the creation of God; I know thy works, that thou art neither cold nor hot: I would thou wert cold or hot. So then because thou art lukewarm, and neither cold nor hot, I will spue thee out of my mouth" (Revelation 3:14-16).

> If I am 100 percent given to the service of my Lord, then I can be content wherever I am.

The option to be a fifty-fifty Christian isn't there. Throughout God's Word we are called to make a clear and defined choice. There is no room for a fifty–fifty attitude.

What about my culture? Oh, there are some things we do and some traditions I wonder about, but overall I like the Anabaptist/Mennonite way of life. I also admit, with Laura, that sometimes in a moment of frustration I may wonder what "another" life would be like, but not as a serious thought. I am far too blessed. The benefits of living the way we do are beyond anything I could explain in one simple story.

If I am 100 percent given to the service of my Lord, then I can be content wherever I am. My surroundings don't matter as much as the choice within my heart.

I can embrace my culture or I can be discontented. It is totally up to me. I can build up or I can tear down. I wasn't born into a Hutterite home, but I was blessed to be born into a Mennonite one. If someone asked me the same question I asked Laura, what would my answer be?

I want to be like Paul and say, "For I have learned, in whatsoever state I am, therewith to be content" (Philippians 4:11).

I want to be happy right where I am. We can be strong Christians in many different churches. The church isn't salvation; it's the condition of my heart. Jesus is the way to God, and anyone can have a relationship with Him and follow His ways.

Some things about the Hutterite practices made us scratch our heads a bit, but I know there are many folks who may feel the same about the Mennonites.

I really liked Laura. Her sweet smile and contagious laugh blessed me. I hope someday to meet her again—if not on this earth, then one day in heaven.

We may not be from the same background, but with God as our Father, we are all part of the family of God.

CHAPTER TWENTY-THREE

Who Is Your Hero?

Then Peter opened his mouth, and said, Of a truth I perceive that God is no respecter of persons. Acts 10:34

We've all heard of hero worship. It's done all the time in society around us. People elevate sports giants or Hollywood actors and musicians to hero status. The president and those in authority can also become heroes. People fall into hero worship in many ways.

This reminds me of a story.

A young lady was seeking for something more in her life. No matter where she turned, she always seemed to be failing in something or making a bad choice. She would look in the mirror and become discouraged because nothing about her seemed beautiful or nice. She was often irritated and lived with lots of negative emotions.

She noticed an older woman at church who seemed so kind and gentle. "If only I could be like her," she thought longingly. This older woman seemed to have the nicest clothes, her children were dressed to perfection, and every time there was a meal at church, her food was delicious. Everyone at church seemed to like her, even Mrs. M., who didn't like many people.

The young lady's admiration grew, and she tried to mimic the older lady's way of dressing and the way she talked. This woman became the culmination of who she wanted to be; she seemed perfect.

> If you elevate someone to the position of hero, you will be let down.

One day at a ladies' gathering, this young woman overheard a shocking conversation. Two women stood talking, and though she couldn't see who it was, she overheard every word. In stark contrast to what she had always believed, she heard the voice of her "hero" passing on a juicy bit of gossip—and she was relating it in a voice laced with venom.

At home, after the party was over, the young lady cried bitter tears of disappointment. With tears flowing, she spilled the story to her grandmother. Her grandma's words of wisdom followed her the rest of her life.

"Your first mistake was taking a human being and elevating her to God."

The young lady protested that she hadn't considered her like God, but her grandma continued, "We are never being fair to people when we lift them up to a position they cannot possibly hold. No person can be your hero because he or she will let you down. Only God can hold the place of total admiration in our lives."

Those words are so true.

I don't know about you, but I have been guilty of hero worship. Maybe it is a minister we really enjoy or a speaker who intrigues us. Maybe it is someone who can sing well, can write or talk well, or even just dresses right that grabs our attention and admiration.

With little thought, we elevate people to a position that isn't fair. We imagine them as godly and spiritual. We might even try to meet them or see if we can become part of their inner circle, not because we really want to know them, but because we find it elevating to our own status. We love the reaction we get when we say we talked to a certain well-known minister or singer.

Isn't that hero worship?

Remember, if you elevate someone to the position of hero, you will be let down.

Let me share an experience I had.

Visitors stopped in unannounced and my house looked like a disaster zone. It was one of those days that I relaxed when I shouldn't have, failed to pick up where I should have, and left the toys right where they were—underfoot. I could make excuses and say I had a sick two-year-old and was fighting a headache. But that wouldn't change the facts—I looked like a messy-haired, disorganized, frazzled, and unmotivated individual.

I tried to act pleasant and ignore the mess, but that was impossible. I was stifling my horror the whole time. As they headed out the door about an hour later, the woman turned to me with a laugh. "You know," she said, "it's nice to see you are normal like the rest of us." She swung her hand toward my disaster zone. "I always thought since you were a writer, you had it all together."

Ouch.

If I could have, I would have pushed a button and disappeared through the floor. I know I blushed and laughed. "Yes," I agreed, resisting the urge to push some loose strands of hair under my veiling. "I'm just like everyone else—except maybe worse."

After she left, I tried to pull some dignity back in the form of a strong cup of coffee. I thought of my writing journey and the many articles I have published over the years. *Do I really come across as having it all together?*

I sure hope not. If you elevate me to that level and then get to know the real me, you will certainly be disappointed.

I am a normal woman with the same quirks, perks, and idiosyncrasies as everyone else.

And so it is. No matter how many gifts, abilities, or personality traits a person has, no one can live up to hero status for long.

Some people are given positions of authority, which calls for our respect, but they are just as human and fallible as anyone else. We all need God's grace.

In Acts 10:34 Peter says, "Of a truth I perceive that God is no respecter of persons."

In God's eyes we are all the same.

CHAPTER TWENTY-FOUR

Who Am I?

Therefore if any man be in Christ, he is a new creature: old things are passed away; behold, all things are become new. 2 Corinthians 5:17

Who am I? Someone recently shared this question with me, and it got me to thinking. Initially, it seems easy.

I am Loura, the wife of Carl. I am a mother of six children. I am a daughter of my parents. I am a woman. I am a friend, an aunt, a niece, a sister-in-law, a homemaker, a seamstress, a cook, a laundress, a gardener, a writer . . .

You could also come up with a list of who you are. But the bigger question is, who are you in Christ?

In Christ, I am redeemed, forgiven, made whole. I am a new creature, His daughter, a recipient of unmerited favor, mercy, and grace. The list could go on to great lengths.

The challenge is to combine these two answers.

Now, who really am I?

I am Loura. In Christ, I am redeemed and made whole. I have given my life to Him; He knows my name. He is the Lily in my valley and my bright and morning Star! But in my weakness, I sometimes talk too much, get impatient too easily, and become discouraged by things out of my control. I am a people-pleaser. I can be weepy and giggly. Satan throws my past into my face with all my failures. But in Christ I am free to claim who I am—His child! Nothing Satan can use against me can overcome Jesus' blood that covers me.

I am a wife. With Christ, I can be submissive, loving, and caring. In my humanness I often struggle with wanting things "my way." Only in Christ can I be the loving wife I want to be. By acknowledging when I have failed and making amends with my husband, I can experience a life-giving marriage.

I am a mother. Because of Christ, I love my children and desire with all my heart to raise them in a godly home. But because of my humanness, I can grow impatient. I become weary of the discipline and the monotony of day after day of teaching, training, and nurturing, especially when it seems to fall on deaf ears. I struggle with anger when things go wrong. If I fail to recognize my weaknesses and continue without repentance, I will pass on my weaknesses to my children. When I refuse to acknowledge my sin, I create chasms of hurt in my children's hearts that could push them from the Lord. Only in Christ can I truly be a godly, loving mother.

In all these areas of who I am, there are both strengths and weaknesses. Yes, I am a friend. But am I a good friend—a trustworthy friend? Do I reach out and care for my friends when they are hurting? Am I willing to take time to stop in and encourage someone even when it interferes with my plans for the day? Are my friendships all about me, or are they about connecting in a way that brings all of us to a closer walk with God? Only in Christ can I be the friend I truly long to be.

The same with being an aunt, a daughter, a daughter-in-law, and a sister-in-law. Only in Christ can I show the love and compassion I truly want to show. In my humanness, I will fail. I will forget. I will say the wrong things at the wrong times. And too often I will be selfish. Only in Christ can I be who He wants me to be.

> By choosing to focus on who I am in Christ, I can seek the Lord's help to overcome my failures—one step at a time.

We are daughters of the King! I think of Acts 17:28: "For in him we live, and move, and have our being." By choosing to focus on who I am in Christ, I can seek the Lord's help to overcome my failures—one step at a time.

Because of Him, I can be victorious. Not because of who I am, but because of who I am NOT! I am not a servant to sin. When I choose to follow Christ, I choose a life of denying myself and following Him. I am no longer bound by sin and Satan. I can claim freedom in Christ! But only because of Christ.

He is my hope, my joy, and my salvation!

In Christ, my true identity far outweighs my humanness. Praise Him!

CHAPTER TWENTY-FIVE

Memories, Nostalgia, and Home

For the Lord himself shall descend from heaven with a shout, with the voice of the archangel, and with the trump of God: and the dead in Christ shall rise first: Then we which are alive and remain shall be caught up together with them in the clouds, to meet the Lord in the air: and so shall we ever be with the Lord. Wherefore comfort one another with these words. 1 Thessalonians 4:16–18

As I drove through our little town of Landisburg this morning, a rush of nostalgia flooded over me.

I see the bank where I loved to go with Mom as a little girl, hoping against hope the teller wouldn't miss me in the back seat and would hand me the beloved lollipops my children still wiggle for today. Many of the other places are also much the same. The post office hasn't changed in twenty years except having a handicap ramp installed, and the auto body shop still carries the same name though its ownership has passed on to the next generation. The gas station has changed hands since the days I worked there as a teen, but it still looks the same and gives me the same feelings when I stroll through the aisles. The firehouse, though somewhat changed, still has the same appearance of busyness and emanates a feeling of safety and care. And last but not least, I see the little two-room school. It is where I attended as a child, taught as a young woman, and now send my children to school. I have gone from being student, to teacher, to parent, and finally school board member's wife. Oh, the memories, joys, heartaches, and laughter that lie within this little town!

While much has stayed the same over the years, even more has changed. The people who were old when I was little, the men and women who stood around in the local businesses sharing laughter and opinions and fussing over us children, now lie at rest in the graveyards of one of the six local churches.

Yes, there are so many memories here . . .

I grew up on a dairy farm two miles outside of Landisburg—and as I write this, I am only three and a half miles from it. When we climb to the top of the ridge behind our home during hunting season, I can see the buildings of my childhood home. As dusk falls over the land, the twinkling lights of the town in the distance create a feeling of warmth and comfort.

It's all a part of me—the roads whose twists and turns I know like the lines on my hand, the familiar mountainous horizon, the rolling landscape. Though life has carried me in many directions, I have always come back to this place.

Not far from town is the brick church where I first met Jesus.

Now my home congregation has become my children's congregation. The same doctrinal truths that flooded over me as a child now fill their ears. This is the place where my choice of faith led to baptism. My children sit on the same benches where I sat and shed many a tear of conviction, sorrow, and joy. And where I joined in songs of worship with my brothers and sisters in Christ. Now the older ones in the church are my parents, and I have become part of the middle-aged group. I went through stages where I didn't appreciate this church as I should have, but now I can't imagine life without it. As we go through joys and sorrows with these people, I realize they have become family.

I love these places my heart calls home. Though not perfect, it is a comfortable fit that spells *home* in the perfect way. To use the drive-through at the bank and know the teller well enough to ask about her daughter who is struggling with MS—and to be able to recall when that daughter was a little pigtailed girl. To stop at the local pizza place and meet an older neighbor who knows not just my husband and me, but also my parents.

When we were first married and settled in this area, I was afraid the people wouldn't know my husband. Now he is probably as well known as I am because he does a lot of local work. He has become friends with the neighbors I grew up with.

Not too many women have the experience I have—to raise my children right where I was raised.

So what makes this place home? Is it the buildings? The landscape? Our home? The people?

To me, it is all of the above.

I long for my children to find this area as charming and peaceful as I do. Oh, I don't have to look far in my memory files to find some unpleasant ones, but today I choose to focus on the positive memories, leaving the not-so-pleasant ones with the past. Everyone has some unpleasant memories; that's part of the world we live in. No one's growing-up years are pain-free and totally peaceful. But why should I wallow in the negative when God has been incredibly good to me?

Each of us has a choice, and today I choose to see the beauty of God's blessings.

I challenge you to do the same. No matter where life has taken you, what pain lies in your past, take time today to look for the positives. Pick out the memories that fill you with warmth and joy. It will do so much for your outlook.

As I crest the hill overlooking my favorite valley and turn toward home, I wipe the tears from my eyes. Yes, I love where we live.

But as much as I feel at home here, I long for that real "homegoing," when I enter my eternal home. When my address is no longer McCabe Road, Landisburg, but a Royal Street in heaven, only then will I truly be home.

It won't be the streets of gold or my new body that make it home for me. Nor will it be the tearless eyes or even the sweet embrace of never-ending love. It won't be the meeting of family, friends, and loved ones—as much as my heart wants this. It won't even be the glory and the peace in that beautiful place.

The Apostle John says, "Behold, the

> The real moment of ecstasy will happen when the spirit within me connects with my Maker, my Best Friend, my JESUS.

tabernacle of God is with men, and he will dwell with them, and they shall be his people, and God himself shall be with them, and be their God. And God shall wipe away all tears from their eyes; and there shall be no more death, neither sorrow, nor crying, neither shall there be any more pain: for the former things are passed away" (Revelation 21:3-4).

The real moment of ecstasy will happen when the spirit within me connects with my Maker, my Best Friend, my JESUS. When I step into the embrace of those Everlasting Arms, when He holds me and says those words of welcome.

Then I will be HOME.

To stay.

Oh, glorious day!

About the Author

*L*oura and her husband Carl make their home in the beautiful rolling hills of Perry County, Pennsylvania. Loura enjoys a cup of coffee on the patio in the misty morning while being serenaded by the many birds that make their homes in the surrounding woodlands. Many a writing project has been birthed in these quiet moments with God as the sun filters through the treetops.

Married since 2001, Carl and Loura have been blessed with six children—two boys and four girls—which makes these quiet morning moments even more necessary. As a young girl, Loura remembers English and literature as her favorite subjects in school. Writing has become a therapeutic way to process the many emotions that come with being a mother. You may recognize her writing from *Ladies'*

Journal and *Keepers at Home* magazines.

Loura's greatest joy comes from being a child of God, a wife, a mother, and a homemaker. She is also a bookkeeper—and an author in the moments between. She enjoys people and would love to have you stop in for a cup of coffee. If you wish to contact Loura, you may email her at clnoltfam@gmail.com or write to her in care of Christian Aid Ministries, P.O. Box 360, Berlin, OH 44610.

About Christian Aid Ministries

Christian Aid Ministries was founded in 1981 as a nonprofit, tax-exempt 501(c)(3) organization. Its primary purpose is to provide a trustworthy and efficient channel for Amish, Mennonite, and other conservative Anabaptist groups and individuals to minister to physical and spiritual needs around the world. This is in response to the command to ". . . do good unto all men, especially unto them who are of the household of faith" (Galatians 6:10).

CAM supporters provide millions of pounds of food, clothing, Bibles, medicines, and other aid each year. Supporters' funds also help victims of disasters in the U.S. and abroad, put up Gospel billboards in the U.S., and provide Biblical teaching and self-help resources. CAM's main purposes for providing aid are to help and encourage God's people and bring the Gospel to a lost and dying world.

The Way to God and Peace

*W*e live in a world contaminated by sin. Sin is anything that goes against God's holy standards. When we do not follow the guidelines that God our Creator gave us, we are guilty of sin. Sin separates us from God, the source of life.

Since the time when the first man and woman, Adam and Eve, sinned in the Garden of Eden, sin has been universal. The Bible says that we all have "sinned and come short of the glory of God" (Romans 3:23). It also says that the natural consequence for that sin is eternal death, or punishment in an eternal hell: "Then when lust hath conceived, it bringeth forth sin: and sin, when it is finished, bringeth forth death" (James 1:15).

But we do not have to suffer eternal death in hell. God provided forgiveness for our sins through the death of His only Son, Jesus Christ. Because Jesus was perfect and without sin, He could die in our place. "For God so loved the world that he gave his only begotten Son, that whosoever believeth in him should not perish, but have everlasting life" (John 3:16).

A sacrifice is something given to benefit someone else. It costs the giver greatly. Jesus was God's sacrifice. Jesus' death takes away the penalty of sin for all those who accept this sacrifice and truly repent of their sins. To repent of sins means to be truly sorry for and turn away from the things we have done that have violated God's standards (Acts 2:38; 3:19).

Jesus died, but He did not remain dead. After three days, God's Spirit miraculously raised Him to life again. God's Spirit does something similar in us. When we receive Jesus as our sacrifice and repent of our sins, our hearts are changed. We become spiritually alive! We develop new desires and attitudes (2 Corinthians 5:17). We begin to make choices that please God (1 John 3:9). If we do fail and commit sins, we can ask God for forgiveness. "If we confess our sins, he is faithful and just to forgive us our sins, and to cleanse us from all unrighteousness" (1 John 1:9).

Once our hearts have been changed, we want to continue growing spiritually. We will be happy to let Jesus be the Master of our lives and will want to become more like Him. To do this, we must meditate on God's Word and commune with God in prayer. We will testify to others of this change by being baptized and sharing the good news of God's victory over sin and death. Fellowship with a faithful group of believers will strengthen our walk with God (1 John 1:7).